VIGILANTE

Published by TRUE LIFE CRIME BOOKS
www.truelifecrimebooks.com
info@truelifecrimebooks.com
First published in paperback 2010
ISBN 9 780956839107
British Library Cataloguing-in-Production
Data:
A catalogue record for this book is
available from the British Library
Typeset by Marc McLean

VIGILANTE

BY

CHARLIE SEIGA

ABOUT THE AUTHOR

BEST SELLING AUTHOR OF KILLER, THE HYENAS, A STREETWISE KID and THE JELLY GANG

Charlie Seiga was one of the most dangerous men in Britain. Men were murdered in and around the city of Liverpool, and many times the police marked him out as the killer. The killings were swift, brutal and brilliantly organised. The victims; liberty takers and sadists, were all hard bastards who dealt in the most vicious kind of violence. He was born 1940 in Huyton, Liverpool 14. Growing up after the war years times were hard, particularly in the late 40's and early 50's. Kids went hungry and food was rationed. Some families had to beg, steal or borrow to survive. There seemed no way out for some kids; but Charlie found his own way out. On a routine basis; together with his childhood gang, they did what they had to do; providing food to put on their families tables amongst other things.

IN 1952 Quote from Charlie: *'My life of crime began after I had a vicious street-fight with another kid. He was the local hard-case bully; he and his gang used to way lay me and my two friends. My friends and I were good little earners at that time, and because they couldn't make anything themselves, the hard case bully used to force us to hand over any gear that we had on us. It was like a sort of mugging that goes on today. He was bigger and older than me; aged 15, but I fronted him up and made a mess of him. That gained me the respect of all the local street kids, and I became a gang leader; I was just 12 years old!'*

AT THE AGE OF THIRTEEN he meets his mentor a woman of thirty-eight years old, her name is Winnie. With Winnie, Charlie progresses further, she has him well groomed and dressed as an office boy wearing blazer and shirt and tie and she teaches him how to steal expensive diamond rings from under the noses of high class jewellers. This was well planned out, displaying real classic cases of robberies which were highly rewarding.

IN 1954 at the age of fourteen and with his young villainous gang they committed crimes that would put a professional criminal to shame, and he became one of the richest teenagers in the city of Liverpool, where they operated from.

1955. At fifteen years old he eventually gets caught for a jewel heist and even though he is a juvenile he still gets severely treated and interrogated. Police methods were ruthless in those days. He was taken outside in the freezing cold winter rain and handcuffed to a cast iron drainpipe for hours all because he refused to sign a confessed statement. Eventually he was remanded to a juvenile remand home, where he witnessed the sexual abuse of young boys; by their carers, who liked to be called Master or Sir. Charlie rebelled over what he had seen, and due to the subsequent uproar he caused in the remand home he was finally released on bail and, ironically, all charges against him were dropped.

Quote from Charlie: *'Before arriving at Woolton Vale juvenile remand home, I had heard all kinds of stories from kids on the outside about what went on there. Some of the staff were beasts. At night in the dormitory it would sometimes happen. One of the staff would come in pretending he was just saying goodnight and then select one of the little kids and the filth would start. Some of those kids were only about nine or ten years old. The beatings I witnessed were terrible too. How these people got these jobs was beyond me. Those days, forty-five years ago, everything was 'hushed up' and it would be twenty years before the outside world faced up to the problem and accepted that for decades it had been the kids telling the truth and the wardens and staff who had been lying. I knew then that nobody would believe the kids if they complained. I was fortunate nobody tried anything on me...maybe it was because I was bigger and older and could handle myself.'*

1956; aged sixteen Charlie turned more and more into a young gangster; but a gangster with a difference. One who will grow to live by his code of honour. He hates women beaters and child molesters. His presence becomes a constant challenge to the lowlife that prey on those who cannot defend themselves.

1957, at the age of seventeen he mastered the art of safe blowing; which at the time was considered the pinnacle of excellence amongst the top criminal fraternity; and they gave him their respect. He was eventually arrested and remanded to an adult prison. As the crime was serious and high profile; high-ranking police officers from different parts of the country where safe-blowing crimes had taken place, came to interrogate him, (which in those days, was very severe), but he refused their requests to talk.

At the High Court in the city of Chester, he stood charged with this serious offence. The right honourable Mr Justice Castles; who presided over his case, was quoted as saying: 'He is like a young lion who had tasted his first blood.' But through a legal and a technical point at the trial, the seventeen year old Charlie Seiga walked out of the court free, and made history for being the youngest safe-blower in Great Britain!

In 1964 at twenty-two years of age, he served a prison sentence of two years in Walton Prison, Liverpool. It was alleged he was dangerously armed with a shot gun; it is said he kept a gang of men including a police officer at bay, whilst his gang escaped.

QUOTE FROM CHARLIE: *'To be honest when I entered the prison I had acquired a massive reputation, it gained me respect amongst the top cons, so with a bit of pull here and there I was given a cushy job.'*

He was appointed work on the prison reception. One of his duties was to serve meals to the last person in Britain to be hanged! He recalls seeing the condemned prisoner (his name was Allen) arriving back from court having been sentenced to death, being taken to the condemned cell, and being the last person to speak to him.

QUOTE FROM CHARLIE; *'I remember saying to Allen 'You'll be ok, you'll get your reprieve.'* He seemed confident *because six months before; a man named Masters was in the same condemned cell and he got reprieved. Also at that time in 1964 capital punishment was about to be abolished.'*

Allen though was unlucky...he was hanged!

On the morning of the hanging all the prisoners in Walton Prison went from uproar to complete silence. We all knew that he was dead. After about an hour all our cells were unlocked; a friend of mine who was a cleaner told me he had been ordered to clean out the condemned cell; he told me it had been in a terrible mess there were blood stains on the walls and some of the furniture was broken. Later on one of the screws told us that Allen had put up a ferocious fight. I believe what used to happen was that if the condemned man struggled or tried to resist there would be a gang of screws as a back-up, who also assisted the hangman.

IN THE LATE 1960'S AND 70'S Charlie became one of the most successful villains of his time. Police believed he was the brains behind the major firms involved in bank raids, wage snatches armed robberies and other serious crimes involving hundreds of thousands of pounds, but they remained unable to convict him; he became known as the 'Houdini' of the criminal underworld.

IN THE 1980'S AND 90'S, crime had rapidly changed, the old school type gangster had almost disappeared, a new breed of criminal had emerged; and the vast majority of these became ruthless in their activities. The gun became; and still is, the weapon of choice. Gangster wars had broken out amongst the criminal fraternity!

IN 1998 he went on trial for murder; he was accused of pumping three bullets into the head of one of these new lowlife breeds. He had also been questioned over other killings which were swift, brutal and brilliantly organised.

QUOTE FROM CHARLIE: *'It is quite true that I have been accused of killing other men and questioned about unsolved contract killings; the Liverpool Murder Squad; in their eyes still believe I was responsible. But they are wrong.'*

QUOTE FROM THE TRIAL JUDGE: *'This is a classic case of a contract killing.'*

He was acquitted. No one has ever been convicted of the murder.

CROWN COURT
Regina V Charles

Particulars in Support of Reg. 9 (5) (B)

This was all in all as gruelling and hard-fought a murder trial as any I can remember in my 27 years at the criminal bar, in which time I have defended in literally dozens of important murder trials. This was a trial which demanded long hours of preparation at nights, weekends and in the early mornings in my hotel room to prepare for cross examination.

It was a dramatic and even a thrilling case. Nobody present will ever forget its atmosphere or the scenes of pandemonium in the public gallery which accompanied the final not guilty verdict.

This trial lasted 19 working days in all and I have to say I underestimated both its length and factual difficulties at the outset. This was, in summary, in the very top league of contested murder trials in this country.

Jonathan Goldberg
3/11/98

CONFIDENTIAL POLICE MEMO

Liverpool Police Force 1998

Charles Antony Seiga – D.O.B. 7/4/1940

Charlie Seiga had a reputation for being a violent character. Intelligence was constantly being received of shootings being perpetrated by this man, but rarely would anyone come forward to complain about him.

He was known to be a careful planner and always seemed to provide a back door for himself when he knew he was to be arrested. He would often disappear after such events, and when the heat died down, would calmly walk into a police station and give himself up, knowing full well that the complaint had either been withdrawn or that the complainant, through fear, had been bought off.

He would vent his violence on other criminals who harmed or tried to bully his family or friends.

Having left the police force and now retired, it came as no surprise to me when I read about Seiga being arrested for a contract killing. How he got out of that one I do not know, and the secret of that job, along with many others, will no doubt be carried with him to his grave. The police are not looking for anyone else in relation to this matter and, in my experience; they must be more than satisfied that they had the correct man in the dock.

He was commonly known as Charlie Seiga, but we had another name for him - Killer!

Charlie Seiga became the longest reigning gangster in Great Britain; stretching from the 50's right up to the late 90's. He retired from a life of crime a few years ago; he is now reformed and a successful crime writer.

For Karen
A lady in every sense

I would like to make a dedication to the ordinary man or woman in the street that has suffered an atrocious experience at the hands of this modern day lowlife scum.

CONTENTS

PROLOGUE

COURT 2006

Quote from the Honourable Justice from my trial:
'John Christian the jury has unanimously found you guilty, and in my opinion it is the right verdict. You not only committed the cold-blooded murder of three young men, but you were also involved in other atrocities. Those charges are to be left on file. Our courts will not tolerate this so called 'vigilante justice' in this country, it can cause anarchy and God knows what else. I sentence you to life imprisonment, with a recommendation that you serve no less than twenty five years.......Take him down.'

The judge in his so called *masterly* speech did overlook some important points when he was summing up to the jury. He was in my opinion, biased. He did not mention that the three young men the prosecution portrayed, who had been shot and killed, were crack cocaine addicts and also known rapist, who went around terrorising people on the said council estate from where they operated. Then again it wouldn't get mentioned in court simply because it's what is known as undisclosed evidence. This evidence could prove vital for my defence, but it is always kept under wraps. In other words it's up to the police or crown prosecution service to use their own discretion. Of course, they very seldom do let it be revealed, simply because it could help the defence and sway the jury to acquit.

In that same courtroom only weeks earlier, before my trial began, a man, sorry I won't call him a man I'll rephrase that; a 'beast' is more appropriate, was standing trial for sexually abusing a child. The judge, who was the same judge that presided over me, let the paedophile walk free from court even though he pleaded guilty.

Quote from the same judge: -

'It would not be in the public interest to send this man to prison; he will be placed on probation for a period of two years, with strict guide lines for medical purposes.'

We are all led to believe in our country we have the best law in the world. That may well be so, if the law is practiced right and above all fair... but is it?

I am forty nine years old; I must serve the minimum of twenty five years out of the life sentence I have just been given. Add that to my age and it will take me right into my seventies, which is by today's standards an old man.

Can I get through this hell that I am about to endure? To be locked away in a prison, year after year, with no prospect of ever being set free?   I don't think so; the way I see it; I'm already a dead man.

A WAY OF LIFE

My name is John Christian. I was born in my mother's bed on a council estate called Wood Green somewhere in Liverpool. I won't go on too much about my family tree or background, except to say that I and my two younger brothers, Mark and Vincent, had a fairly comfortable and happy childhood growing up on our estate in the late 1950's and 1960's. Family values, such as manners and respect for our elders, where imperative to the core. If we kids didn't to the line and got a bit out of hand, for example being unruly etc, we were chastised by our parents in some way or another.

A vast majority of other kids' parents were like ours, they too disciplined their children if they didn't behave themselves. My mother and father were from a working class background, my dad worked on the Liverpool docks for most of his life and my mother, who incidentally was a good mother, was very clean and decent. She stayed at home taking care of the children and the house. It's funny when I look back and remember all those mothers or housewives in those days. To me, they all seemed forever doing something in or around the house, cooking, cleaning, shopping and minding their kids. The man of the house, who was known as the 'bread winner' in those days, was always out working; that's of course if there was any work for them. For some of those men who didn't go to work or simply couldn't because there was no employment for them, their means of support was doing a bit of this or a bit of that, meaning they were '*at it*.'

Life was very hard at times, especially for those families who had lots of kids to support; for them it was a struggle to make ends meet. Most of the time the people who were in that hard-up situation had no choice really and went and got themselves involved in what we called the 'other business' (making a few quid illegally).

In a way could you blame them? The wages the working class people were paid in those days were a pittance compared to now. So when I'm talking about people breaking the law by making a bit on the side, it was in a sense accepted by the rest of the neighbours.

This illegal business that people got up to actually benefited the community, as any ill-gotten gains that were sold on our estate were always knocked down to half price. Poor working class people welcomed these sought after little luxuries, clothes, electrical goods, food, cigarettes and so on. On most of the council estates at that time, there was always a very strong close-knit community, people were sociable and talked to each other, they also shared compassion for one another. If one of our neighbours was having hard time, other neighbours would rally around and try to help out. It was also very safe in those days, nobody worried about shutting their doors, and you could more or less walk into anybody's house and feel welcome. Nobody stole from their neighbours, it was practically unheard of.

Men and women, young or old, were never intimidated; children could play out in the street and feel safe. Maybe it was this way because of the rules we had amongst ourselves. We had golden rules, which were very seldom broken. If on the rare occasion those rules did get broken and the person or persons found responsible were found out, well it was God help them! They would be severely dealt with, and I don't mean by the bizzies (police). Most of the men that lived on the estates got it sorted themselves.

People actually 'Sheriffed' their own communities. That's the way it was. Today everything is so different; things have taken a turn for the worse. Loyalties and family values have almost disappeared. A major breakdown in society has descended, and everything has spiralled out of control. The police can't seem to resolve anything; they're fighting a losing battle and are completely demoralised. Now the streets have become lawless. Criminal gangs are roaming the streets and are committing the vilest of acts imaginable; rapes, violence on the old and infirm, arson attacks on family homes, gun crime and senseless murders.

Unfortunately, some decent hard working people still live amongst it all. They feel trapped and can find no way out, it is an unbearable existence for them. Nobody calls the police; people are too frightened of being labelled a grass. The ones who *have* reported crime and asked for help have deeply regretted it because of having to face a backlash of reprisals from the marauding street gangs. These drug-crazed gangs of lowlife scum have no morals whatsoever; they would think nothing of setting fire to a woman's house even if there were babies inside. These low-lifes have no compassion at all. So this is now the way of life on most of these council ghettos.

I went back to the Wood Green estate where I used to live, it was the first time in over twenty years; I wished I hadn't. It is now a depressing hellhole of a place. Everywhere was vandalised, it resembled a war zone, but worse was to come. Little did I realise that by going back I found myself in a situation a person could never imagine. I went on a trail that took me to the homes of old people, men, women and children, where I actually saw first-hand the injuries what those gangs of sick degenerates had inflicted upon them. After witnessing and seeing some of the old neighbours living in fear and too terrified to go out of their doors, it got to

32

me. I knew then that something had to be done. My belief was; those who intimidate these unfortunate people should be intimidated themselves, in a more frightening manner, so brutal that I could guarantee they would never do it again.

If you wonder why a man would choose to take the path I did, getting myself involved in the most brutal of violence, then maybe when you have read my story you might understand.

THE STORY

It all began 18months ago; I had just been released from prison after serving a 10-year sentence. Before I got sent down my friends and I were into crime, some of the moves we did were heavy. We were villains, gangsters, or whatever else they called us all those years ago, but there was a difference to our type of crime compared to most of today's criminals; we never went beating up and robbing old pensioners or terrorising women and kids. The friends who I grafted with at that time were men of decency; we all had strong principles and respect. Stretching from my early twenties until my early forties life seemed dead sweet to me. I had a nice home and a beautiful wife and daughter. My three friends and I at that time where what we call 'bang at it.' Money was coming in thick and fast, but the faster we got it the quicker we spent it. We lived expensively and had a good life style, but, as the saying goes, all good things come to an end.

A couple of days after my forty second birthday I came badly unstuck on some graft I was supposed to be involved in. I was charged with conspiracy to rob a security depot. I won't go into all of the details. My friends never got a pull so they were safe; I ended up getting whacked with a ten stretch. That's the way it went in the game I was in, you played for high stakes and I knew if I were to lose, the sentence would be high. At the time I thought it was harsh what they dished out to me, but it had to be done and I made up my mind up to do it the best way I could. First rule was to keep out of trouble by having no conflicts, staying fit was another priority, and keep my mind focused on different interests such as books and education etc.

I could see light at the end of the tunnel and with good behaviour I could be back home with my family in just under six years. But sometimes things don't go that smoothly, no matter how hard you try. I had done just over three years of my sentence when my beautiful, so-called loyal wife threw the towel in on me; she filed for divorce. It hurt; I knew I had lost everything: her, my child and the lovely house I had bought. I didn't contest the divorce; I didn't want anything back, what was the point? To me it was finished. When the hurt I was going through eased off a little, I thought, why think negative, there's no way I'm a defeatist, I will get through all of this lot, finish my time off and get out of here. I won't go into the boring routine existence of prison life, because to me stories that have been written and told about being banged-up in prison all sound the same.

After serving just under six years, the day of my release finally came around. I walked through those prison gates to be greeted by two of my loyal friends, Jimmy and Paul, together with my younger brother Vincent. Jimmy was the first to grab hold of me. Jimmy was 50 years old but he still looked fit and powerful. This man could really handle himself when it came to any sort of conflict, but right now he has hold of me in a bear hug. 'Hiya John mate, thank fuck that's all over with.'

When he finished hugging me I felt as though my ribs had been caved in. Jimmy was such a loyal friend. Years before when we were at the 'other business' you could rely on him a hundred percent. He would never leave you, no matter what. Paul was the next to greet me, he wasn't as powerful looking as Jimmy, in fact he was completely the opposite, a lot slimmer, but again, still fit looking. Paul was always kind of shy and quite spoken and his manners were impeccable. He smiled and put his hand out to me, he squeezed my hand tight.

'I'm made up for you John, it's about time.'

Paul and I go back a long way together, to when we were just kids. I nodded to him in appreciation; he was one of the gamest men I had ever met in my life. Years ago he proved himself time and again, if something was going down really heavy Paul would be the first one to jump in. A top man all the way.

My younger brother Vincent, he too put his arms around me. Alright kid,' my brother said, 'I'm glad you're coming home. Our Mark is out of town, but he told me to tell you that he is on his way, and he will join up with us all tonight.'

'That's ok Vin,' I said. 'Just drive me away from this place.'

Jimmy butted in laughing and said. 'Yeah come on let's do one away from here.'

We all got into the car. Jimmy sat in the front with our Vincent who would be doing the driving. The car we were in was a cool looking BMW 5series sport. It was a hot summer's day at the end of August. I was just about to take my jacket off inside the car when the air conditioning kicked in, making the drive more comfortable. On the drive home we were all having a good chat. Jimmy turned around to me and said, 'how do you feel now John, coming away from that piss hole you were in?'

'I feel absolutely brilliant Jim,' I said.

'You will feel even better tonight. We have got a welcome home party set up for you.' He started laughing as usual. 'Oh we've also got a stunning looking bird lined up for you. Haven't we guys?'

Now I'm supposed to be dead happy being a free man again, and I was in a way, but there was something nagging at the back of my mind, it was that same gut feeling I had had in the prison. I thought once I was out of the place it would go away but it hadn't. It was her; my ex wife, I didn't think I was over losing her and my baby daughter, (I kept forgetting my daughter wouldn't be a baby anymore; she would have been nearly thirteen years old). I often wondered what she would look like. It had been nearly seven years since I last saw her. They had both moved away from Liverpool many years before and had gone to live down south somewhere. There's an old saying that time is a great healer, but I'm still hurting over it all.

We had been driving and chatting for nearly an hour when the sign of a motorway service station came into sight. My brother Vincent said. 'Does anyone want a drink or anything?'

I quickly interrupted as we were only about half an hour away from Liverpool. 'We might as well carry on, we're nearly home now.'

Jimmy butted in. 'I could do with a leak, but it can wait.'

So we all agreed to keep going.

It's funny, I thought to myself, when I mention home I immediately think of Liverpool; the city where I was born and grew up, the city I love and always will. For me there's no other place on earth like it. Most of the true Liverpool people (scousers) are warm, friendly and good hearted, but then like every other city in this country; you get the bad element in some way or another.   Paul suddenly jostled me out of my thoughts.

'We're almost there, John.' He said.

We were driving along the East Lancashire road, (or the Lancs as we scousers call it) the road heads into Liverpool. We had driven from up north and we were now less than ten minutes from the city centre.

'I hope you like the pad we've got you kid,' said my brother. 'It's very spacious and has two bedrooms.'

Jimmy turned his head around to me. 'Yeah it's well decked out inside, the furniture we got and everything is all set up in there for you.'

I nodded my gratitude. 'Thanks Jim. And you Paul.'

Paul just nodded and patted my shoulder. 'No worries John.' He said.

This is the way it was with our circle; we stuck together through thick and thin. All of those years I was stuck inside, I often thought about these two men, Jimmy and Paul. Their loyalties were just beyond compare; they had always been there for me without fail. Coming up to see me on the prison visits for years, they had even got things sorted on the outside when I needed it, and now the two of them along with my brothers had bought me an apartment. Of course my brothers had never let me down, but they were blood, they too had finished with the other business (crime) I was glad to hear. It was a dying trade anyway, that sort of old school crime, which was once our way of life. Now they had all settled down and had got their own legitimate businesses.

'Here you go John, take a look at our old neighbourhood.' Jimmy said looking out of the car window.

I too looked through the car window. We were slowly passing a field to the left of us, looking across it we could see the council estate named Wood Green where we all grew up. I couldn't believe what I was seeing. Some of the houses where boarded up, some had no roofs on them and you could plainly see that in the past they had been set on fire. The field were we used to play football and mess about when we were kids had burnt out cars on it. I thought; I'm glad my mother and father never saw any of this. They had long passed away. 'What the fucks happened over there, Jim?' I asked.

'It gets worse if you go inside the place.' My brother said.

'It's supposed to be a *no go area*,' said Paul.

Jimmy started laughing. 'Even the bizzies (police) are shit scared to go into the place.'

'I didn't know it was that bad,' I said. 'It must be well over twenty odd years since I last paid a visit there. Are any of the old neighbours still living there?'

'Yeah there's still the odd one or two,' Jimmy went on. 'Do you remember that girl Carol? You know John; the one you used to do a bit of hanging out with when we were kids?'

'Yeah.' I nodded.

'Well I bumped into her when I was coming out of the newsagents over there. It must have only been a couple of weeks ago. We got talking for a few minutes and your name cropped up.'

'How was she?' I asked. 'How did she look?'

'She lives on her own, the same house she was born in, her mum and dad's house, but her mum and dad are well planted.'

'Carol was a stunner when we were in our teens,' I said.

'Don't go there,' Jimmy said. 'She looks terrible, and I mean, I know she is touching the fifty mark but she looks older. She is disabled and on a walking stick, she told me she was beaten up and mugged by a gang of kids.'

Vincent interrupted. 'That's what it's like now kid,' he said. 'Scumbags running around causing all kinds of havoc.'

Jimmy told me he went on the estate to see his nephew who was in some sort of conflict with a gang of scallies. It appears they had smashed in the windows of his girlfriend's house, so Jimmy's nephew went out hunting them. It turns out he got two of the gang, but he lost it

42

and went to town on them both with a wooden pick axe handle, putting the pair of scumbags in a bad way. He thought there might be some come backs from the rest of the gang, so Jimmy got wind of it and showed up with a few handy fellas and got it sorted.

'We're here,' my brother announced. 'Here's your new home kid, what do you think?'

The car had pulled up outside an apartment block in the city. All four of us had got out of the car and were stood there looking at the apartments.

'I'll let you know when I see the inside.' I told my brother smiling. 'No I'm only joking kid, I'm dying to see the layout, come on lets go in.'

My brother passed me the car keys; he said the apartment keys were on the same ring as the car. I began trying to take off the apartment keys, after having a bit of a struggle I finally manage to get them off the car ring and I passed the car keys back to my brother. Then my brother passed them on to Paul, Paul then passed them to Jimmy. The three of them seemed to be acting a bit silly to me. They all looked at me grinning.

'Here,' Jimmy said throwing the car keys back to me laughing.
I caught the keys.

'The BM goes with the pad John.'
I shook my head holding on to the keys.

'The four of us bought it for you the other day, kid,' my brother said smiling.

'Look, this is just brilliant, thanks a lot guys.' I said. I was just overwhelmed.

Paul came and stood facing me; he put his two hands on both my arms and held them tight, looking me straight in the eyes.

'John what you did for me and the rest of us all those years ago, I will never forget. We should have been doing that bird (prison) not you.'

Jimmy nodded and said. 'Yeah John, you were dead sound, you carried (took the rap) for us mate.'

I took Paul's hands away from me, and I said to them all. 'I didn't do that for rewards from you, you should know that.'

'We all know that kid,' said my brother Vincent, 'but this is all given to you with a good heart nothing else.'

We all ended up inside the apartment. It was a penthouse on the top floor, and as they said it was spacious, trendy and had good river views, I couldn't have asked for anything better.

It was decided that we should all meet at my brother's house for a homecoming celebration. By now it was late afternoon; Paul and Jimmy were to pick me up around eight o-clock, that was giving me plenty of time to get myself sorted and everything.

I wanted more than anything to get a hot bath with plenty of Dettol and soap in the water, followed by a good hot rinse. I felt as though that prison smell was clinging to me. Once that was done I could then relax and chill out.

After relaxing for a while, eight o'clock finally came around. Paul, Jimmy and my other brother Mark came to pick me up. Mark was the youngest out of our family, being in his early forties. He was beaming all over his face when he saw me.

'I'm sorry I couldn't be there on the pickup J. I'm made up you're out at last.'

Here was a brother who idolised me when we were kids, it was always 'our J this and our J that', but anyway, our Mark was another one who was doing very well for himself these days.

The home coming party they had for me went off ok; it was the usual routine, a lot of shaking hands and hugging etc. Jimmy's nephew, young Steve introduced himself to me; he was a fit looking kid in his early twenties. We struck up a conversation and I instantly took a liking to him, he seemed fairly intelligent and talked a lot of sense. Although he was years younger than me, I found we both had a few things in common; he didn't drink much, he had no bad habits and kept himself fit and healthy too.

As the evening wore on, the conversation had turned to the run down Wood

Green council estate we had all lived on years before. Unfortunately, Steve still lived there. He poured his heart out to me explaining in detail what it's like living amongst some of the vilest scum you could imagine. He went on to say he is determined to leave the place. He and his girlfriend are buying their own house shortly, away from it all. I asked him.

'Is the estate as bad as people make it out to be?'

He then revealed to me what really went on over there, the things he told me made my blood boil. Women were getting molested on a regular basis; old people were forever getting beaten up and robbed. At one point during the conversation he told me of a young kid about twelve who didn't live on the estate but who came to visit his gran. One of the gangs ambushed him in broad daylight on the street; they stripped off the clothes he was wearing, even stealing his training shoes, all because they had a label on them. Not being content with that, they went and took things further; they slashed the poor kid with a knife badly disfiguring him.

'Didn't anyone get the bizzies onto it?' I asked.

'You're fuckin' joking aren't you; the bizzies are a waste of space, they haven't got the bottle to come into the estate.'

I just shook my head in total disgust. He went on to say that he and two mates tried to curb it.

'You know, we tried to look after our own, but there's just too many of those scumbags to sort out.'

Jimmy came over and joined in the conversation. 'I've told our Steve to get the fuck out of the place, the sooner he leaves the estate the better. He is fighting a losing battle. Otherwise he will end up in jail for doing one of those animals in, or worse still, getting himself killed.'

The party had started to whittle down; people were saying their goodbyes and wishing me all the best as they were all departing. Steve and I exchanged phone numbers. I told him as soon as I got settled in I would be going over to the estate, it would be in a few days. I was going to go to see Carole an old lady friend of mine.

Everybody had left the party, it was now the early hours in the morning and there was only our own crowd left, Jimmy, Paul and my two brothers. We were all still talking our heads off. We mostly talked about the past and what we used to get up to, such as the things we had done and everything. By this time I was really shattered but still feeling good, because I was in the company of people who I loved and trusted, my brothers and best friends. Jimmy was sitting opposite me; he leaned forward in his chair and said.

'John, we have all been waiting for this day to come around. We are all over the moon to have you out with us again. While you were inside the four of us have all been doing well as far as the graft goes, by that I mean we are all legit now, but anyway the four of us are putting you on an income. We...'

'Hang on!' I interrupted. 'You have all done enough for me; I'm starting to feel embarrassed about all this.'

Paul butted in, 'John, I know what your pride is like.'

Then our Vincent chipped in. 'Kid whether you like it or not you're going to get a wage. At least until you get back on your feet again.'

I just looked at them all, not knowing what to say. My brother went on.

'Look kid, me and Mark have our own distribution company, Jimmy and Paul are into the property business, and the four of us have all agreed you should be involved. So you're going on the books and that is it.'

'And if you don't like the idea you can fuck off back to jail,' said Jimmy, laughing his head off.

Then they all laughed.

'I really appreciate this; it seems too much for me to take in.'

We then went on talking for another hour or so, until finally, I said. 'I need to get my head down, I'm really done in.'

We eventually all decided to split. Our Mark and I got a taxi back to my apartment, he got his head down in the spare bedroom and I got into a clean soft bed for the first time in years. I don't know what happened to the girl I was supposed to be with at the party, I think she got pissed off or passed out. I have been without a woman for almost seven years, another day or two won't make much of a difference. I turned on my side, the pillow was soft and comfy under my head and within less than a minute or so I had crashed out.

When I opened my eyes the next morning my younger brother Mark was standing at my bedside, he was smiling down at me. At first I thought I was dreaming. Then he said.

'Are you ok kid? I'm sorry I had to wake you up'

I realised, I wasn't dreaming. I was really there, and free. I rubbed my eyes taking everything in and feeling absolutely brilliant. 'Yeah, I feel great,' I replied.

'I have to step on it,' my brother said. 'Me and Vincent have to attend a meeting shortly. We have to see a couple of prominent businessmen. You don't mind do you kid?'

'No, that's ok Mark, you go ahead with whatever you have to do,' I said.

'Sound, we'll catch up with you later on. Oh and by the way,' he said just as he was going out of the door, 'that bird who you were supposed to be with at the party has been on the phone a couple of times, she asked if you would give her a ring, her phone number's on the table. I think she's doing her nut, she said you fucked her off last night.'

He started laughing and then closed the door behind him as he left.

THE VISIT

It was a few days later; about four in the afternoon, when I decided to pay a visit to see Carol. I have known Carol since I can remember, we both went to the same school when we were just little kids and from the age of fourteen to seventeen she was my steady girlfriend. As time went on we drifted apart and lost touch with each other, I think because my family and I moved away. That was twenty five years ago, but right now here I was driving down one of the main streets inside what is now referred to as a ghetto. The street, our street, the one I lived on, is the next turning on the left. I still can't believe what I am seeing, how bad this has deteriorated over the years. It looks a right piss-hole of a place. I have just a sharp left turn to do before I am in the right street, but I suddenly had to jam on my brakes, coming to an abrupt halt. Right in front of my car was a gang of scallie kids, altogether there must have been about six of them; two of them were sitting on bikes and they were making no effort to move out of my way.

They all look about fourteen to sixteen years of age. I sounded my car horn. One of them put his finger up to me with a sneer on his face; another one of them had pushed the front wheel of his bike in front of my car. He was bigger than the rest of them, wearing a hood; it looked as though he was challenging me for a fight. I started getting out of my car and the cheeky little pricks were still standing their ground. I stood up and snarled at the one with the bike

'Get out of the fuckin' way twat,' I said.

I could tell by his attitude he was the main one out of the gang. I stepped forward and wrenched his bike away from him lifting it up to my head I slung it on to the side. By now I was in a bit of a temper, one of them had shouted to me.

'Alright sted-head there's no need for that.'

I think my appearance gave them a jolt and their bottle went a bit. I am almost six foot, pretty thick set and dead fit. The one who I took the bike from said, 'hey mate what's your problem?'

He spoke to me with a no-respect attitude that started to put me on one. They were overlooking the fact that I know these streets like the back of my hand and I know how to talk real street talk.

I put my face right up to his and said, 'listen to me cunt. I'm from this street myself and the problem is this; you and this gang of pricks get out of my way right now, otherwise I will do the fuckin' lot of you in.'

He nodded. 'Ok, ok, don't be goin' off on one!'

I got back into the car and they all started to move out of the way. One of the little no-marks who was wearing a hood, was defiant to the last. Just as I was about to drive away he put his hand up to me as if he was holding a gun, and shouted. 'Next time, bang!'

Now I completely lost it and I went fucking mad, I rushed out of the car to cop for him, but the little prick ran away. One of the others shouted to me.

'Leave it out mate, he's just fuckin' about that's all.'

I thought to myself, I'll be here all day the way things are going so I decided to let it go. I got in the car and drove off.

Thinking about that minor conflict I had just had, it's a good job I controlled myself, as things could have got blown out of proportion. Worse still, I could have ended up back inside (prison), all because of that gang of uncouth scallies who had no manners.

Incidentally, *'sted head* is street-slang, meaning on steroids or the juice. These days a lot of young men resort to this, by injecting themselves with steroids. It's not only unhealthy to do this sort of thing, it is also very dangerous. It pumps their muscles up quicker and bigger. It's a way of cheating really. The men that use this method are not doing a real workout, hence those kids thought I was 'juiced up' when they saw my appearance, but they got it very wrong. I'm not into that crap or any of the other chemicals that some young men of today take.

I'm just about to pull up outside Carol's when my phone rang. It was Steve; Jimmy's nephew.

'Hiya John. How you doing?' He asked.

I told him I was alright, and that I was on his estate about to knock on Carol's door. He went on to tell me that somebody has told him a gang has just tried to hijack a new BMW car.

'It wouldn't be you by any chance would it?'

'No way,' I assured him. 'It was just a confrontation with a few no-marks who wouldn't move out of my way, so I sorted it.'

I told him I would give him a bell later on. I got out of the car and knocked on Carol's door.

Old memories quickly flooded back to me; almost thirty years ago Carol and I were just two clean living teenagers in love. At that time in our young lives we didn't have much as far as money and things go, but we were young and dead happy, both of us making plans for the future. She was stunning, with long blond hair and blue eyes, all the boys in the neighbourhood wanted Carol but I was the lucky one.

After a few moments the front door of Carol's house opened, she stood looking at me, holding the door handle with one hand and a walking stick supporting her in the other hand. When I saw her appearance it threw me, I tried very hard to conceal my shocked emotions. She was in her late forties being the same age as myself, but she looked years older.

'Hello Carol,' I said smiling at her. 'Don't you remember me?'

Her eyes opened wider. 'Oh my God,' she said. 'John I don't believe it's you?'

We both went inside the house, it was a typical council house built around the early 1950's; there was hardly any hallway, a small front room and a kitchen at the rear. Upstairs there would be two or three small bedrooms. Inside, the place had the look and feel of the 1970's regarding the decor and furniture etc. Carol started with difficulty to sit down in one of the armchairs and I sat down on a small sofa opposite her. After a few minutes, and after some small talk, Carol started pouring her heart out to me.

CAROL'S STORY

Carol was an only child. She got married when she was twenty-five years old, and together with her husband had moved away from the estate. She never had any children of her own and as time passed her marriage had broken down. Her mother had lost her husband and was living on her own in very bad health, so Carol came back to live with her. Most of the old neighbours had passed away themselves and others had left the area to live elsewhere. Carol's mother eventually died, leaving Carol on her own and she became a sort of recluse, the only time she ever left the house was to go for a bit of shopping. She did have a little dog for company but that was about all. At the beginning of 1990 things started to change for the worse around the neighbourhood. Younger families where moving in, some with gangs of kids and the place seemed suddenly turned upside down. The noisy racket of loud music getting played at all hours and screaming arguments, with some families fighting each other. It was and still is, a living nightmare. I looked across at Carol, the walking stick propped up at the side of the chair.

I asked her softly, 'what happened to you? Jimmy told me you had been mugged and badly hurt.'

She bowed her head shaking, and then broke down sobbing. I felt dead sorry for her, I went and sat down on the arm of her chair and put my arm around her.

'Come on,' I said. 'Come on love, I'm here for you. I need you to tell me what really happened.'

I finally got her to pull herself together, then after a little while she revealed everything to me:

Apparently, the lowlifes who live around here thought she had money or valuables in her house, but she didn't, in fact she had absolutely nothing at all. Carol's only ever been a working class women. She went on to tell me a gang of four scumbags smashed her front door in one night. They quickly over powered the small women of seven stone (brave bastards aren't they) and tied her up. The little dog she had was a Jack Russell and while all the violent activity was happening, the dog kept running around and barking at them. One of the scum was armed with a hammer, he grabbed hold of the little dog by its collar and picked it up towards him. Carol was lying back in an armchair, then this horrible prick who had hold of the little dog leaned towards her and demanded to know where her valuables where. She couldn't tell him simply because there was no valuables. He then, with full force, smashed the skull of the little dog right in front of her. The poor dog was twitching its life away. The scumbag hung it on a coat hook on the back of the kitchen door. The other three scumbags had started ransacking the house looking for anything that was sellable. After killing her little dog, the one with the hammer turned his attention to Carol. She started screaming hysterically, he started to beat her punching her in the mouth and face and screaming at her, unconvinced that she didn't have anything of value.

'Where's your stash? Come on tell me, where's your fuckin' stash?'

This animal then takes it further he starts to smash her knees in with the hammer; by now Carol has practically passed out. She told me she couldn't remember anything after that brutal hammer attack. Quite soon after this horrific attack she was taken by ambulance to hospital and the police were called. It seems that the four scumbags had gone, leaving her half dead, but they couldn't close the front door behind them when they were leaving, because of the damage they had caused to the door when they first gained entry. It wasn't long after that a passer-by, seeing the smashed door open, came to investigate, and the rest is history.

As I listened to this terrible ordeal she had been through it made my blood boil. I just don't know what happened to my mind after listening to that. I was seething with hatred for those animals. I wanted more than anything in the world to hunt them down and make a mess out of them, but I had to control myself in front of her. Although this brutal event happened to her almost two years ago, I could see she was still badly traumatised. Her poor mind was messed up. I asked her one more question and she told me what I wanted to hear.

A few weeks after the attack, one of the scumbags was arrested, he got caught trying to sell some of the small belongings he had taken from Carol's house. He was charged with the violence on Carol and stealing from the property, but the solicitor who was defending him found a loophole in the case, and through a few technicalities the violent attack charge was dropped. He pleaded guilty to the lesser charge of handling stolen property. In court he got a walk over, but he wouldn't get a walk over with me because I would get right on his case. I would hunt this animal down and by the time I had finished with him he would never use any of his limbs again.

I quickly changed the subject and hugged Carol, assuring her everything was going to be alright from now on. I told her I would get her a mobile phone so she could phone me anytime whether it was night or day, and if any problems arise I would be with her in a matter of minutes.

She looked at me, her once beautiful face was so messed up; her left eye socket had been badly damaged leaving her with a slight disfigurement.

It broke my heart looking at her this way.

'John,' she said. 'When we were kids I always felt safe with you and I know even now you will be there for me.'

I nodded. 'Yeah I will always be there for you Carol, no worries.'

I stood up and stroked her hair and kissed her cheek. Let's face it, who on earth could she turn to, there was nobody else who could help her, and as for the bizzies; well they were just a waste of space.

Before leaving her house I asked her. 'Are there any of the old neighbours still living around here?'

'Yes,' she said. 'Do you remember Frank, the man who used to tell us all off for being naughty when we were kids?'

'Yeah,' I said laughing. 'Frank. Frank Cook. That was his name. He must be well past eighty now.'

It was very true, what Carol had said, if kids on our street ever did get out of line it was Frank Cook who would be the one to tell us all off. He would never raise his hand to us, but he just had a way about himself, and we as kids all respected him. He was a big dark haired powerful looking man who always smoked a pipe. I remember we used to play in the street kicking a ball around and if the ball went into Frank's front garden he would pretend to go mad and keep it on us, but about ten minutes or so later he would give the ball back to us all. He loved his front garden, it was always full of lovely flowers and it was his pride and joy. He could do anything with his hands, everybody in the neighbourhood went to Frank especially if something was broken and needed mending. There has been many a time when you would see him sitting on the sidewalk outside his house fixing a kids bike or repairing a wheel on a girl's pram. He was the heart and soul of our community and his wife Mrs Cook was a lovely woman, she would often come out of her house carrying a tray of homemade cakes and biscuits for us kids. Frank and his wife never had any children of their own; I think because of this they sort of adopted every kid in the street.

Carol went on to tell me that he still lived in the same house at the very end of the street. She also told me his wife had died a couple of years ago and he himself was now in the poorest of health. I had been in Carol's for what seemed like hours; it had started to go dusk outside. I looked at the time and it was almost nine o'clock so I said my goodbyes to Carol assuring her that I would get things sorted within the next few days. I thought the first thing on the agenda was her house. I would make it like a fuckin' fortress, new locks and bolts on the window and doors, no harm would ever come to Carol again I would make sure of that.

I pulled away from Carol's house in my car, all the talking I had been doing over the last couple of hours had made my mouth dry, and I felt dead thirsty. I just realised; I never had a cup of tea all the time I was in her house. So I thought before I visited Frank I would drive to one of the local shops, they were only a couple of streets away. After a few minutes I pulled the car up outside of a row of shops. There was an off-licence open, which was next door to a chippy that was also open. Gangs of kids could be seen outside both premises messing about and as usual causing a nuisance. Their ages were between fourteen to about maybe sixteen or seventeen. As I got out of my car a few of them were clocking over at me, I walked over to the off-licence and had to brush past some of them to gain access to the premises. Inside of the place a few more kids were in there being a nuisance, the counters had steel mesh grills all around them and reaching up to the ceilings. Behind the grills were two very frightened looking staff, a man and a woman, they were Asian or Indian, I think, I couldn't be too precise about their nationality but any way they looked very, very nervous. When I spoke to the woman who was doing the serving, the gang who were messing about went a bit quiet. One of them was a girl about fifteen and the language coming from her mouth was disgusting. I asked the woman for a cold drink, and as I was being attended to three lads about sixteen to seventeen came in the place. They were the same ones who I had to brush past at the entrance to the shop. The three of them were talking very low to one another, sort of mumbling between themselves. I then asked the woman for a half bottle of brandy, it was for Frank, I also asked did they sell pipe tobacco. When I mentioned pipe tobacco the three lads burst out laughing and the girl who was standing with the three lads said very loudly.

'Fuckin' pipe tobacco ee...yak.'
I turned around and looked at the fowl mouthed bitch with disdain, and then turned back around to the woman who was serving me.

One of the three lads shouted over to me. 'Hey mate that pipe tobacco is crap. We'll sell you some good skunk.'

Then another one of the lads shouted. 'It goes down well with the pipe.'

They all burst out laughing again. I paid for the goods and walked to the door. Just as I was about to leave another one of the lads shouted to me.

'Is that your beama?' He was pointing to my BMW car.

I nodded. 'Yeah.'

He went on. 'Dead boss motors them aren't they mate?'

64

The man who was behind the shop counter seemed to have plucked up some courage and asked them all to leave the premises. Just as I was walking out of the door, the young unruly girl shouted back to him,

'Fuck off you Paki bastard!'

Then one of the three lads shouted to him. 'Yeah we'll smash your fuckin' windows in.'

I spun around and shouted to the lad.

'Hey you.'

He looked at me.

'Yeah you,' I said looking at him. 'Just cut it out.'

He then goes and spits on the shop floor trying to look hard and thinking that will impress me. His two mates started looking at me, sort of sizing me up, I thought to myself; 'the three of you just fuckin' try it on', but nothing came of it.

I got in my car and looked at the two shops before driving off. I noticed that the chippy was Chinese. I looked at the gang outside; it had got bigger. I thought to myself; 'I bet the Chinese who work in there have all kinds of abuse to put up with too'. Come to think about it those two shops are giving this community a good service, more so the off-licence and newsagents which are combined. I mean that Asian couple must have to open between 5am and 6am every morning until last thing at night and that would be seven days and nights every week. To me that's very hard graft, I wouldn't fancy doing it, not only do they do all that hard work, but what about all the abuse they have to contend with night after night?

A couple of streets later I had pulled up outside Frank's. Frank's house had been one of the neatest in the street, it was always kept nice and clean and tidy, but what I am looking at now is total carnage. The place was like a tip, broken bottles and rubbish strewn across a once lovely garden. I noticed one of his windows boarded up and graffiti depicting filthy and abusive language sprawled right across the bricks of the house. I was just about to walk up the small pathway of his house, when two teenage lads came riding erratically on their bike along the sidewalk.

Suddenly the bike they were on hit a woman who was walking by. She fell over just a couple of yards from where I was standing. The lad who crashed into her screamed,

'Mind out of the way you fuckin' old bitch.'

They then just carried on riding away leaving the woman lying there. I went and helped her to get up from the floor. She was a bit shaken. I asked if she was ok and could I give her a lift home, but she insisted that she would be fine and brushed it off as if it was a regular occurrence around here, she then hurried away. I went and knocked on Frank's front door and waited for him to open it, but there was no response. So I bent down and shouted through his letterbox, 'Frank, Frank!'

I heard a bit of movement coming from inside and an old croaky voice shouted. 'Who is it?'

I told him who I was and he answered back to me. 'Is that really you John?'

'Of course it is Frank, now come on, open the door.'

I heard the sound of an inside bolt being unlocked and the door finally opened. Frank stood there half hunched over a Zimmer frame, his appearance seemed to have shrunk in size, and his face looked gaunt and white. I couldn't believe he was the same man I knew years before.

I put on a brave face for him with a smile, 'how are you doing Frank? Carol the girl who lives at the top end of the street told me you still lived here.'

I stepped inside the house and started closing the door.

'I'm ok son, except for this arthritis. I don't think I would be able to get about only for having this frame to help me.'

He slowly lowered himself down into an armchair.

'Here you go Frank.'
I passed him the bottle of brandy and the pipe tobacco.

'That will take your aches and pains away. You will be throwing that Zimmer frame away and running around like a young whipper-snapper,' I said laughing.

His old face lit up.

'Aw thanks John. You haven't rob....'

'No Frank. I haven't robbed them.' I said laughing.

He was thinking back years ago. When I was a kid I used to do a bit of pilfering now and again. I always remembered amongst other things to wizz some pipe tobacco for Frank. When I used to give it to him he didn't like the idea of it at all, but I always had a way to persuade people. I still do to this day.

'Come on Frank,' I said pointing to the bottle of brandy he was clutching. 'Have a drink it will make you feel better.'

'Yeah, ok John,' he said. 'Will you have one with me?'

I don't touch the stuff myself, but how could I refuse?

'Of course I will have one with you my old mate. Where do you keep the glasses?'

He pointed to an old glass cabinet. 'There's some in there.' He said.

I went over to the cabinet and took out two glasses. On the top of the cabinet I noticed two old photos, in silver frames, one of the photos was of a good looking, fit, young man dressed immaculately in a Royal Air Force uniform. He had jet-black hair slicked back, and a thin pencil moustache. It was signed 1945. It was Frank. I poured out the drinks and passed one to Frank, I then picked up his photo in the frame, looking at it more closely.

'I'll tell you what Frank, you looked the part there didn't you mate?' I said indicating to the photograph.

He nodded at me with a smile. I then looked at the other photo. It was of a young, pretty woman; his wife Hilda. I said to him,

'Your wife Frank, Mrs Cook, was a good woman. I remember when were all kids, how she looked after us all. She practically fed all the kids in the street. I'm so sorry to have heard she has passed away Frank. Carol told me she had a heart attack.'

Just then we could here loud shouting and banging coming from the house next door, it sounded terrible.

'I think they're having a bad argument next door Frank.'

Frank started to tremble in his chair. It was so sad to see him like that, he seemed as if he was wasting away. The noise that was coming from next door started to get a lot louder, I think a fight was starting to take place. I peered through Frank's window and sure enough a man and a woman who were surrounded by some of their kids were screaming and shouting at each other. I had parked my car between both houses, so I decided to move it around the corner just in case it got damaged. I told Frank not to panic.

'I'm going outside to park my car away from the commotion.'

After I had parked up I came back and let myself back into Frank's.

'Come on mate,' I said. 'Take no notice.'

I poured him another brandy then surprisingly; I poured one out for myself.

'Let's have a drink and forget those scruffy bastards next door.' I was trying my best to cheer him up.

Frank suddenly blurted out to me. 'It wasn't just a heart attack that killed my Hilda, John, it was those young evil bastards.' He started pointing to the front door. 'Out there.'

'What do you mean Frank? Who out there? What's been going on? I've noticed two of your front windows are boarded up and there's all kinds of graffiti on the front of your house. Frank, don't keep it all bottled up, tell me all about it mate. I know what you're like regarding your pride; you used to drum that into me years ago. *Don't ask anybody for help son, always try and do it yourself.* Those were your words to me Frank.'

'I don't really want to tell you John. You might kick off and make matters worse, and I don't want to see you going back inside.'

'Frank, come on, tell me. I promise you, I won't get myself in any trouble.'

After my persuasiveness he finally opened up to me.

OLD FRANK'S STORY

'It all started with these gangs that are just out of control, it is a living hell what we have to put up with. I opened my front door one morning and all my garden plants had been ripped up and thrown all over my pathway. They even stole my wooden front gate, my garden ornaments, a wooden wishing well, a bird table and a windmill. My wife Hilda loved them all. I did phone the police and they came out a couple of days later. Can you believe that? The police said they would make some inquiries with the neighbours, but nothing came of it. Then things started to get worse, it got so bad that the gangs were banging on my front door and windows every night, my wife and I were getting no peace or sleep at all. It was because of me reporting it to the police, which of course made matters worse, as they then started shouting 'Grass, grass' through my letter box each night and we had our windows smashed in. I have been broken into four times now; God knows when they are going to try again. They have given Hilda and me a dog's life.

The first time we were broken into, Hilda and me were sitting watching TV; it must have been about ten o-clock at night, when our front door was smashed in. Three thugs, all wearing hoods walked into the room with a kind of swagger. One of them calmly walked over to the television set and started to unplug it. My wife and I started to protest, I mean, I've turned eighty years of age and I know I have no chance trying to have ago back at these bastards. My Hilda stood up and tried to ask them nicely, I remember her saying to the thug,

'Don't take that from us son, that television's all we've got, we haven't even finished paying for it yet.'

The animal just comes over and punches my wife right in the face. She fell down on the floor and he starts shouting to her, 'I told yeah to shut your fuckin' mouth up.'

I went over to try and help my wife, but one of the other thugs turned on me, he started to beat me up. After he finished, he asked me.

'Were do you keep your money eh? Come on tell us you old fucker.'

He started to search my pockets whilst I was lying on the floor. He took sixty pounds from me, which was in three twenty pound notes. I remember him waving the notes and laughing, shouting to the two others,

'Look what the old fucker had on him.'
I tried to reason with them.

'That's all we have, that's our house keeping money.'

My wife again tried her best to talk to those animals but it was to no avail. Me and

Hilda were still on the floor then one of them bent down he grabbed Hilda by her hair and pulled her face towards his saying.

'Listen you pair of old fuckers; I'm warning yeah... no bizzies. Alright?'

The two of us nodded 'ok'. Then he said they 'would come back and burn this fuckin' place down if you think about getting the police'. They finally left but my poor wife was in a bad state of shock and her face was badly bruised. I did try my best to comfort her. We didn't go to the police over it all, my wife was too scared of reprisals, and besides what is the point asking the police for help? They are never around when we want them.'

Frank paused from the story for a few moments.

'I think they have sorted their grievance out next door it's gone very quiet,' I said.

I could see by his old face the torment he was going through, he looked so frail and helpless, it was killing me to see a man I once knew to be so big, strong and proud reduced to this. I gave him another tot of brandy and decided to have one myself, I thought I better had, the way I was feeling right then. I had a little jovial chat with him, trying my best to cheer him up. The trick worked, he sort of relaxed and composed himself. He then continued with his story, only this time he seemed to have gained more confidence in himself. I think it was a sort of therapeutic thing with him getting it all off his chest. When all's said and done, this old man had been more or less isolated in his own home with nobody to confide in for so long.

He went on to tell me that the same gang came back twice more; they didn't even break the door down this time.

'They used to just knock and make me open it for them. I had no choice really; Hilda was terrified of them. They would come in and bring cans of beer with them, just sitting around and causing us all kinds of heart ache, smoking, swearing and taking drugs. They would always leave about five or six in the morning taking with them some of our belongings. The last time they came was a complete nightmare there must have been about five of them they all clambered out of a van parked outside my house. It was the same routine just barging in on us and causing all kinds of mayhem.

After them being in here for a few hours the dirty evil bastards started stripping our house bare, they even took the little fridge we had. I was more or less begging them not to take it but they just laughed at me. My wife was heartbroken after this time and I decided we must get help from the police, but they told us they could do nothing without evidence. I vigorously protested to the police, I asked them – what about their fingerprints that were all over my house, isn't that enough evidence for god sake?' The police told me point blank, no. Simply because it was in a statement I had made to them that I allowed these scum bags inside my property for drinks and socialising. I explained to them we were both intimidated by these animals and that I had no choice but to allow them into my home. The police weren't having any of it, although some of the bizzies were sympathetic towards us both, but according to them they cannot proceed with their inquiries. They had been notified by the crown prosecution to discontinue, in other words; the evidence is not strong enough and it would just be thrown out of court. The last and only advice the police gave us was for my wife and I to leave the area, but where could we go?

About six months after that terrible ordeal we had both been through, I buried my wife! It was a heart attack she died from, but I know it was that evil scum out there that had caused it all.

The day my Hilda's funeral took place my house got broken into, I don't know why they targeted my home again, because there was nothing left in there to steal, except they found my old medals which had been presented to me after serving in the R.A.F during the second world war. That robbery was reported to the police but yet again the police said they had nothing to go on. They *did* advise me to have my house more secured, especially of a night time, because that's when the yobs are roaming about more often. A representative of the housing trust came to visit me, and good enough, they had locks and bolts fitted on my front and back doors. I am glad in a way they did, because now I have been getting verbally abused and stones thrown at my windows some nights. The gang who are doing this seem a lot younger than the last lot that used to come around. Again, this is all because I sought help from the police. Now I'm getting labelled a grass all over again. So as you can see John, I am now virtually a prisoner in my own house.'

When Frank had finished his story I started to pace up and down. I was fuming with hatred for these lowlife degenerates when I thought about what they had reduced this decent person too. Let's face it; here we have a man; a good man with an impeccable character who served his country during the war. Frank was highly decorated for his bravery flying planes over enemy lines and risking his life for what? To be reduced to this; being tormented and intimidated? It's not as if he was young and fit and could take care of himself, no, he was an old man in his eighties. I calmed myself down a bit after pacing up and down. I looked at my watch; it was half past ten. I told Frank I would have to be making a move as it was getting late. I felt a bit guilty having to leave him, as he looked so vulnerable. I did reassure him I would definitely be back tomorrow to get a few things sorted out; I thought I could also call on Carol. Just as I was ready to leave Frank's house I could hear a bit of a commotion going on outside. Thinking it was those noisy next door neighbours again I looked out from behind the curtains. It wasn't the neighbours but a gang of about four or five teenage lads standing around the front of Frank's house, one of them was drinking from a bottle. I turned to Frank, who by now was starting to tremble. 'Who are these Frank? Are they the bastards who have been tormenting you?'

He just nodded his head. 'They're not worth getting in trouble for John. They will most probably go away shortly.'

The noise outside was getting a lot louder, the gang then started to chant in unison. 'Grass, grass, grass!'

As the chanting was going on, my main concern was for old Frank now. I persuaded him to stay in the back kitchen of his house; I sat him down in the chair reassuring him everything will be ok. Having done that, I noticed an old type of sweeping brush with a long thick wooden handle propped up against the wall of his kitchen. I grabbed hold of it and snapped the pole in two. It was just the right length - about two and a half foot. I thought this would do me just fine. I started making my way to the front door when there was a loud bang, one of the thugs had thrown a glass beer bottle against the door.

Loud laughter could be heard coming after it. That's when I completely lost it, I ran to the front door wrenching it open and at the same time clenching the wooden handle in my hand. The gang of scum were startled and went dead quiet; they didn't expect to see the likes of me there. I screamed at them.

'I'll kill the fuckin' lot of you.'

I ran towards them and they all started scattering down the street, with me running after them like a raving lunatic. Determination was driving me on; I wanted to do the lot of them in. I did manage to catch one of them, I grabbed hold of the little bastard by his neck, the others didn't stop, not even to help one of their own. Proving that they had no loyalties, even to each other. They carried on running like the rats they were. I had dropped the wooden staff I was carrying so I smacked him across the head a couple of times with my hands, but he was a slippery little rat and he got away from me. He eventually ran and caught up with the rest of his pack, they were waiting at the far end of the road. They had all regrouped and started to get a bit braver shouting to me

'Come on. Lets have it. Come on, we'll fuckin' stab yeah.'

I picked up the wooden stick and went trotting towards them. They all ran away shouting their threats to me, but nothing came of it. I stopped chasing them and went back to

Frank's house still fuming. I told Frank I couldn't leave him on his own here tonight; he would be at the mercy of those scum dogs. I wouldn't forgive myself if anything happened to him, so I decided to stay the night. I made a phone call to young Steve. I explained to him what had happened and asked if he could call around to take my car to his place for the night. After I finished speaking to Steve I was just getting things sorted with old Frank when we both heard a loud knock on his front door. I thought; 'those cheeky bastards have come back and this time I will finish it!' I went to rush for the front door but Frank shouted.

'No John, take it easy, it's the police.'

He had been peeping through his curtains and had seen them come up his pathway. I composed myself and opened the front door. Two bizzies where standing there with the little yob who I had caught earlier on.

'I see you have got one of them.' I said.
They said nothing back to me, but stood there on the broken glass from the bottle that had been thrown earlier on, then one of them turned to the yob and asked in a stern voice,

'Is this the man?'

'Yeah that's him,' the little rat blurted out. 'He had a big stick.'

The other policeman said to me,

'this young man alleges that you assaulted him by beating him around the head with a stick.'

I could not believe what I was hearing. Apparently what had happened when I had got back to Frank's was; the police were patrolling around in their car. The gang of rats who I had had a confrontation with got a routine pull by these policemen because they were spotted running.

I looked at the little rat, who by the way, was smiling and looking smug between the two bizzies. I leaned myself forward, towards the little scum bag. 'Oh, so now it's you that's the grass? Not that poor old man in here, who you and your gang of no marks have been calling and tormenting each night.'

The little rat shouted back to me. 'It was you who beat me up with a stick; you think you're dead hard.'

One of the bizzies interrupted and asked me had I been drinking he said I smelled strongly of alcohol. I told them, 'yes, I have had a glass of brandy with the old gentleman inside the house.' I then said to the little scumbag.

'Why don't you tell the truth hey? You and your gang of scumbags have been terrorising that old gentleman in there for months. You have even broken into his house and stolen from him.'

One of the policemen said to me that I was making a grave accusation without any proof. I just shook my head in disbelief.

'We are taking this young boy away to the station and if he files a complaint I'm afraid we will have to come back and arrest you.'

With that they then turned and walked away down the path. I shouted after the little rat. 'Go on, make a statement and grass me. I will make sure everybody on this estate knows you are a little grass. You want it both ways, don't you?'

He shouted back to me. 'You battered me and I'm gunna get ya done.'

I went back into the house slamming the door shut behind me.

Not long after the policemen had gone, young Steve turned up. He had brought a friend with him; he was about the same age as Steve, mid-twenties, and very fit looking. His name was Carl. I explained to Steve what had happened regarding the incident I had just had with the little scumbag and the two bizzies. I also went on to tell him what these gangs of scum had been putting old Frank through. The three of us started discussing the situation about what's going on, on the estate. The more we talked to each other the more we seemed to be on the same wavelength, and it connected the three of us. Steve told me that he and Carl were forever having it off with some of these gangs of no marks, but because there were only two of them they couldn't take the lot of them on, and it was only a matter of time before they themselves would come unstuck. In other words, there were too many of the bastards to sort out. It was getting very late by now so we decided to split for the night. I suggested we all make a meet tomorrow afternoon. They both agreed and we decided it would be at my place.

Before they left Frank's we shook hands and I gave Steve my car keys so he could park my car by his place for the night. I just had a feeling my car would get vandalised if it was left here, or the bizzies could come sniffing around and that was just what I could do without - any police harassment. When they had left I shouted up to Frank who was in his bed. I told him I was getting my head down.

I didn't get much sleep on Frank's settee that night; the neighbours who lived next door had music blaring away most of the night. Frank was dead right about them, being inconsiderate bastards. I just lay on my back thinking about what it must be like to live in an environment as bad as this place. Things started going through my mind about it all.

The following morning Steve called around with my car, I offered him a lift back to his house but he said there was no need as he only lived a few streets away and that he would be going on his morning run before he and Carl go for their work out at the gym. It appears they both own a lady's and gent's gym and also an upmarket health shop in the city centre. I thought to myself, no wonder they both look fit and healthy. Steve left and said that he and Carl would catch me later on. He then turned and started jogging away down the street. Before I left Frank's house I got a few things tied up with him and Carol, I bought them a mobile phone each, telling them if any problems arise to phone me at anytime. I told them that I didn't care if it was morning, noon or night I would be there for them no matter what. After doing this I headed back to my place, I needed to get myself sorted and maybe have a kip for a couple of hours.

When I did eventually get back to my apartment that morning I had a couple of phone calls, one was from my two brothers asking me how I was doing and everything and the other was from Jimmy. It seems he and Paul were a bit concerned for me, probably because I hadn't been in touch for a couple of days. Jimmy who is always joking around said on the phone to me,

'John we thought you'd most probably been on a bender with some dirty woman.'

He started laughing down the phone like he usually did. I told him I *had* been in the company of a woman, only it was Carol and also that I had paid a visit to Frank Cook. Jimmy said he remembered Frank and so did Paul. They both remembered him from when they were kids. I then started to explain to them both the situation old Frank was in and also what Carol had gone through, with the lowlife that were terrorising the place. When I had finished telling them, just like I expected, Jimmy shouted down the phone.

'Let's go and sort the scum bags out!'

I told him and Paul to leave it. I didn't want them involved, or my two brothers. I knew they would always be there for me if I ever *did* need any of them. This to me was very personal especially where poor Carol and Frank were concerned.

It was late in the afternoon when Steve and Carl called to see me. The three of us immediately got our heads together discussing how and when we could sort this other business out; it's been going on for too long on our old council estate. Steve and Carl started giving me their views and ways to tackle the situation. I wasn't too impressed. I listened very carefully to what they had to say and after they had finished I had formed my own opinion. Their plans where too erratic and it would only be a matter of time before they would come badly unstuck. Carl and Steve where two loyal game young men who had a lot to live for and I knew that they had been having plenty of run ins with this low-life. Carl's grandmother had herself been viciously mugged in the past, but I said to them, things had to be done differently. So I put it to them; it had to be my way or no way!

I began by saying that what we talk about and plan in this room goes no further. We don't want anything reaching the wrong ears, especially the bizzies. After all, what we were about to embark on was going to be dead heavy. I'm talking about serious violence here. So ok, let's get our priorities right. Number one, any violence that we are about to deal with must be one hundred percent bang on, otherwise we pulled out of it. Remember those scum-dogs would think nothing what so ever about making a statement against any of us, if they were to get badly damaged they would grass us up no problem. More so if it was for criminal injuries compensation they could claim against us. I told them.

'This scum wants it both ways, it's alright for those animals to go around, robbing, beating old pensioners and molesting women, but when the shoe is on the other foot and they get a taste of their own medicine, the rats will start screaming for help. So I'm telling you what we are going to be up against.'

I looked at Steve and Carl, and I said to Carl, 'you are married and have a little daughter.' He nodded to me in agreement.

' Steve you are about to be married.' He nodded too.

'So you can see where I'm coming from. We can't afford to get too erratic or take any silly chances. We don't want to jeopardise anything what so ever, more so for your families. Another main point, and this is very important; we won't ever expose ourselves when we're doing these bastards in. It is imperative we stay ballied and gloved up at all times. One more thing, we all have to stay staunch and loyal with each other, things can be achieved successfully if our strategy is put in to place.'

After I had finished saying my piece Carl stood up and sort of rubbed his hands together,

'Sounds good to me, I'll go along with that?' He said, with enthusiasm.

Steve, who incidentally was a dead ringer of his uncle Jimmy, said. 'Yeah John, I'm well up for that, when do we start? The sooner the better.'

Both Carl and Steve where dead eager to get started so I suggested to them,

'How about this Friday night? We will kick off on that gang of scum who have been tormenting old Frank.'

I knew it was usually the Friday or Saturday nights they started the hounding antics on Frank's house. So we all agreed on that one.

I just wish I could be sorting Carol out first, but getting revenge for her would take me a bit more time if I was going to do it properly. Firstly I would have to find out where those animals lived. My top priority would be to hunt down the one who brutalised Carol with the hammer; my hatred for this animal was burning up inside me.

It was now Wednesday and I made a suggestion to Steve and Carl that we should have some sort of a rehearsal, mainly on how we were going to cop for those lowlife scum. To do the job right we needed to get ourselves a half tidy motor, nothing too big or flash and more important, it has to be down to no one. My preference would be a small van rather than a car; it would be ideal for what I had in mind. Picking one up wouldn't be a problem, I knew a trusted friend who used the right credentials. He could get me any type of vehicle I wanted if need be. Steve asked me.

'Why a *small* van?' Steve asked me. 'I mean a bigger one with more room inside it would be better, don't you think?'

So I explained to him.

'Look Steve, your uncle Jimmy, and the rest of our circle used to be involved in the other business some years ago, as you are most probably aware of, aren't you?'

Steve nodded to me and said. 'Yeah John, I know all about you and my uncle Jim, and I respect you for it, you were all top men.'

'Alright Steve, let me just explain what I have to say to you both. When any of our circle had a confrontation with any other rival gangs;

that is, in our younger days, most of the time we always came off best, and the reason why that was; I always believed in going for the other gangs top man. Take him out and the rest of them would scatter. Now regarding the small van that we will need, it is just for that purpose. If the occasion ever did arise and we would have to take somebody away to sort out properly such as a paedophile or a rapist, one of us drives the van with the body, tied up obviously, in the back. While the rest of us follow behind in a straight motor. You see, it's very seldom the bizzies will ever pull a person driving on his own.'

I paused for a few moments and I could see Steve and Carl fully understood what I was on about. I went on explaining to them that there was no way we were going to have street fights, especially when there were less than a handful of us. There could be ten, fifteen or maybe twenty of them we could be fighting with, plus they would most probably be tooled up with knives and whatever else. No, those sorts of street battles are out of the question. We will keep to our plans and go for their main man at all times, like I have said, get him first and by the time I have finished with the animal it will deter the rest of the scum. Carl spoke to me.

'Hey John, there is one thing we might have over looked, what about all the shootings that are going on? I'm not one for guns, that's all a bit too heavy. I mean I will go around beating up this lowlife all day long with whatever... but the guns, well that's a different matter, if you know what I mean? And another thing, using guns leads to murder.'

'Nobody is suggesting using guns.' I said to him. 'We don't have to, let the scum shoot and kill each other for all I care. No, we don't have to get involved in that side of it, we will just leave that head ache to the police, let them deal with it, if they can that is. Don't get me wrong Carl for what some of these animals have done to people they deserve to be shot.'

After we had been chatting for most of the afternoon we all decided to call it a day and meet up again tomorrow, Thursday.

On the Thursday morning before I met up with Steve and Carl I had been doing a bit of homework. Firstly my good friend delivered to me the van that I had ordered. I had also picked up some equipment that we would need, ballies, gloves, and three wooden pick axe handles. I had also phoned Frank and Carol asking them both if everything was alright? They both told me that so far everything is fine. I mentioned to Frank that I would call on him about half past seven that evening.

Soon afterwards Steve and Carl turned up at my apartment, I explained everything regarding the van and equipment etc, and then we decided to call on Frank. I got the van ready with our equipment intact and the three of us set off heading up to Frank's house.

I drove the van onto the council estate and parked outside a block of flats, which were a couple of streets away from Frank's house. I was the first out of the van with the three pickaxe handles and the rest of our gear zipped up in a golf bag. All three of us entered Frank's house discreetly. By that I mean, I was the first to enter, then Steve was to follow two minutes after me, then Carl two minutes after him. Frank's face lit up when I called to see him but then he got a little bit concerned when I introduced him to Steve and Carl. I soon put him at ease, explaining to him what our intentions were. I told him all the intimidation he had been getting from that lowlife gang had to stop now.

He fully agreed with me in the end, offering his gratitude. We all settled in and sat around having a drink and a good chat with Frank. I could see he was really made up with the company. The things he told us all were so fascinating, especially about his adventures during the Second World War, when he had to fly fighter planes in conflict with Germany. So this was the way the evening was progressing.

We must have been in Frank's a good two hours and in all this time there seemed to be nothing happening outside. There was a bit of a noise coming from the scruffy next-door neighbours, but nothing happening regarding any marauding gangs being around. I looked at my watch, it was getting on for eleven o-clock.

'Have that gang of scum who have been giving you a hard time ever called on a Thursday?' I asked Frank.

'No,' he told me. 'It was usually on a Friday and Saturday and sometimes it could be on a Sunday.'

It was midnight by now and as nothing was happening we decided to call it off until tomorrow. We all left Frank's, telling him we would be back around eight o'clock tomorrow night. We decided to leave our golf bag of tools with him.

Friday night finally came around. Me, Carl and Steve entered Frank's house using the same routine we had the night before. After us all sitting around for a while drinking tea and coffee, time was starting to pass by again. It was getting on for ten o-clock and although there was plenty of noisy activity going on; obviously being a Friday night and all, there was no sight or sound of the young gang of scumbags.

'They might not turn up,' said Steve. 'Their bottle might have gone because of you John, fronting them up last week when you chased after them all.'

Carl thought the same. I was beginning to think they were both right, as it had now turned eleven o-clock.

'Ok if you both feel that way let's call it a night.'

I think they could both see that I was a bit disillusioned over it all, when Steve said.

'Hey John, me and Carl will sit it out all night with you if you want? We are with you all the way.'

Then just as we were about to start making tracks, we all heard a lot of shouting and banging coming from further down the street. I quickly peeped through the drawn curtains, and sure enough, walking down on the opposite side of the street was a gang of about five or six.

'It's them,' I said to Frank. 'I need you to go up to your bedroom and keep your door locked till we have sorted this out.'

Steve wanted to know if we were going to front up to them outside.

'No way,' I told the two of them. 'I have a better idea. We will try and lure them inside of the house, that way no witnesses will see us working them over. I will set up a trap for these rats, and hopefully, with a bit of luck they will fall for it.'

I went and unlocked the front door, leaving it ajar. I just had a feeling about how this lot might perform. They would start off by shouting all kinds of abuse like they usually did and when they got no response from the house they would assume Frank was alone inside. This will give the cowardly rats a bit more courage and if our look is in they will come up the pathway and enter the house.

We all quickly started to put our ballies and gloves on and we grabbed hold of our weapons. Then took up our positions. Steve and Carl crouched themselves down behind the sofa and the armchair, waiting to spring into action. I stayed by the window peeping behind the curtains watching their every move. The noise and the abuse that was coming was getting louder and louder, no wonder poor old Frank and his wife had been so terrified. I was still watching them; they had now entered the pathway and the biggest one of them threw a brick at the front door. The door had moved open an inch or two from the impact. I whispered to Steve and Carl.

'Get ready; they are doing exactly what we wanted.'

They were now outside the front door. Suddenly they went quiet then I heard one of them speak.

'The fuckin' brick has broken the door open.'

Then the same voice said.

'Come on, let's fuckin' steam in.'

They opened the front door and they were now in the small hallway. We needed them to come right into the room where we were lying in wait, one of them shouted,

'Are ya in there grass?'

Another voice said, 'Come on lets go in and fuckin have it.'

They pushed open the door of the room that we were hiding in. They all piled in screaming and shouting: it was at that moment we all sprang from our positions...all hell broke loose!

We began knocking fuck out of them with our wooden pickaxe handles; Steve and Carl (which gave me a bit of a surprise) had both gone berserk with their weapons. They where clubbing them all over the place. Some of them started screaming, two of them got away by running out of the room and out of the front door, literally terrified. I ran out after them, chasing them for a good few yards, but they disappeared out of sight. When I got back on the pathway the rowdy neighbours next door to Frank's came out to see what was going on. It's quite obvious they had heard all the commotion and screams. I still had the wooden club in my hand and my mask on. The sight of me must have scared them to death.

'What the fuck are you all looking at, eh?' I snarled at them.

They didn't reply they just put their heads down.

'Anybody else, including you lot, gives that old man in there a hard time, we will do the fuckin' lot of you in round here.'

They still stood there and said nothing. I told them not to be nosey and to get back in their scruffy house. I glared at them and they just sauntered back inside their house shutting the door behind them. I quickly got back into Frank's. The screams that were coming from the scumbags had now turned into low groans. There were three of them lying on the floor, two of them where well out of it, they looked in a really bad way. Steve and Carl had really gone to town on them. The one who didn't look too badly injured looked up at me from the floor. He was the biggest one, the one who threw the brick at the door. He shouted up to me.

'My older brother and his crew will get you for this. They're gangsters and they'll shoot you. You're all fuckin' dead.'

The prick had an attitude. I bent down to him and said. 'Listen to me you fuckin no mark. I know who you are, we all do, but you don't know who we are. So listen to me cunt. We can cop for you any time do you hear me? One more thing you bag of shit; get that old man's medals back quick, otherwise we're coming back just for you and the next time I get you, I will personally put one right in your fuckin' head. Do you know what I'm going to do now? I'm going to give you a working over you will never forget!'

All the hatred I had for these had built up inside of me when I thought of what this animal and the rest of the scum would have done to old

97

Frank if we hadn't been around. They would have shown him no mercy, and that's exactly what I'm going to do to this breed of lowlife.

I told Steve and Carl to keep an eye out by the window. I jammed a handkerchief into his mouth and I started smashing his limbs in with the pickaxe handle, breaking his arms and legs. I couldn't stop myself, he was practically out, but I went a step further with the violence. Still holding the pickaxe handle I started beating his face into a pulp. His eye socket had gone I smashed all his features away, knocking his teeth out of his mouth, by the time I had finished he was completely unrecognisable. I don't know why, but I really felt so good after inflicting these injuries on him.

'John,' Carl said to me. 'I'm not being funny or anything, but I think you've gone a bit *too* far there mate, I don't think he will ever recover.'

'So fuckin' what?' Said Steve. 'He deserved it. They all do.'

'Alright Carl,' I said. 'If that's the way you think and feel, but remember; this animal showed no mercy on all the old people they have been terrorising.'

There was a brief silence between us and then I said, 'anyway let's drag these scum bags out of the house quick.'

We dragged the three moaning, damaged bodies down the pathway, still wearing our ballies and gloves. The next-door scruffy neighbour came out of his house again followed by a group of his family. I mean even these people who live next door to Frank have been giving him no peace with their unruly ways. I shouted to them.

'Hey, fuck off back inside your house and keep your fuckin' mouths shut, alright?'

He just nodded to me walking back into his house with the rest of his family and closing their door. Funny after all that's been going on in the last few minutes, there was nobody around in the street.

'I will just nip up and see Frank before we get off,' I told Steve.

I ran up the stairs and told Frank to keep his bedroom door locked and not to come out whatever happens. I told him we'd close the front door behind us. I also said to him. 'What you didn't see you can't talk about, alright Frank? So if the police do come around there shouldn't be a problem. After all, how can a frail old man carry out all that violence?'

'Don't worry John, I know the score.'

I said goodbye to him and that I would phone him in the next hour or so. The three of us took our ballies and gloves off. I put them in the golf bag and zipped it up again, we then walked a couple of streets away to where our van was parked. So far so good, everything had gone according to plan. Just before I dropped

Steve and Carl off, I told them, they must destroy their masks, gloves and any other incriminating evidence such as blood stained clothes, shoes etc. These points were extremely important.

'Always remember,' I told them. 'If we do the job properly we will never come unstuck.'

I knew deep down I had no worries with these two young men. They were both intelligent and had good common sense. I thought it would be a good idea not to see each other for a few days, sort of let the dust settle, so we left it at that.

I finally arrived back at my place and after I had got myself cleaned up and sorted a few other things out, such as the van etc. I made a phone call to Frank. It was in the early hours of the morning about two o-clock I was just hoping everything was alright with him. He answered my phone call and relayed back to me what had been going on since we had left his house. Apparently, an ambulance had been called to the scene and some of the neighbours who where gathering around started helping the paramedics to put some of the injured gang members into the ambulance. Frank went on to tell me he had heard a knocking on his front door. He never looked through the window to see who it was, but had stayed up stairs and wouldn't answer it. He said after about twenty minutes or so the crowd of neighbours had dispersed. I asked Frank did any police turn up and he said.

'No, not one. It has now gone very quiet outside.'

I told him not to worry, everything would be alright and I would be in touch tomorrow.

Later that afternoon I had a phone call from Steve, he told me it was all over the evening newspaper about last night's events. Headlining the newspaper, it read:

'Three youths were found badly injured last night; one of them is in a serious condition. According to our sources they were attacked by a gang of masked men. It appears the youths were caught breaking into an eighty year old pensioner's house. The estate where it took place is notorious for its crime and violence. Police reports said the three youths are known to them and they are continuing with their enquires.'

So for the next few days I took things easy and decided to chill out for a bit. The following evening I had a visit from my two brothers together with Jimmy and Paul. We all had a little get together and went to a local restaurant for a meal and a drink. During the course of the evening we discussed the violent attack that had taken place on our old estate. Obviously they were more concerned for my welfare. I got a bit of a lecture from them, in so far as; they don't want me ending up back in jail. Jimmy said to me.

'John, our Steve told me the score and what went on, about the three of you chastising those scum bags. You know what those rats are like; they wouldn't hesitate to make a statement to the bizzies against you. Or could even put a bullet in you, given the chance. So just be careful mate.'

After they had all said their piece to me, and I know it was with good intentions. I told them I just couldn't sit back and see all that abuse that's going on. I went on to explain to them what old Frank had been going through.

'I mean, he looked after us all when we were just kids, and what about Carol? The way she has suffered at the hands of that scum, I have to get that sorted for her. There is no way I can let that go, it's killing me.'

My brother Mark suggested that we all go and cop for the animal, then after we've dealt with him we can call it a day.

'After all John, you can't keep going around trying to sort everybody else's problems out.'

'No', I said to them. 'I want to do this my way and my way only, besides I know how to go about it.'

'John, we will give you that mate.' Said Paul. 'You were brilliant when it came down to organising and planning anything ... remember?'

Jimmy laughed when Paul said that, in fact we all did. The five of us must have been on the same wavelength, thinking back all those years ago when we were 'bang at it' and making plenty in the other business. But that was back then, now things have changed and it will keep on changing as time goes by. I have never been one for looking back, to me it seems pointless. I am always looking forward.

The evening was starting to draw to an end, and after we had finished our meal and everything, it was time for us all to split. When my two brothers and friends had finally left, I decided to hang about for a bit longer. These days' living in the city centre is the place to be, Liverpool is so vibrant. Every amenity a person could wish for is all here in the city centre. The place is just buzzing, and the night-time well that's something else.

So here I was just strolling around, taking everything in. I finally ended up having a coffee in some cafe bar, which was inside a theatre. After a while I got talking to two birds, it turns out they were amateur actresses from a show that was being held at the theatre. We were having a good chat together and I was feeling good being in their company. One thing led to another and the three of us went back to my place for a nightcap. I had to admit they were two stunners like most Liverpool women are. I think they were well into their late twenties or there about. After a while I got lucky, one of them left and one stayed, her name was Tracey.

So I ended up having a pleasant evening and a fantastic night.

The next morning I walked Tracey around to her place. She too lived in the city centre, we both agreed to meet at a later date, but on second thoughts and being in the frame of mind I was in at the time, I didn't want a relationship just yet.

Later that day I phoned Carol and arranged to see her about securing her house. I drove to hers that afternoon with a friend of mine who was an expert at installing alarms and security cameras. My friend and his son both owned a little security firm. He guaranteed me that Carol's house would be like Fort Knox by the time he had completed the work. While I was at Carol's I thought I'd better phone old Frank. I asked him the usual questions like was everything alright? Had the bizzies been to see him? He said the police hadn't been near but there was something else that had happened. I told him I would be at his house in ten minutes.

I left my car outside Carol's and walked down to Frank's. It was only at the end of the street. When I got inside Frank's he gave me feedback on what had been happening with regards recent events. Apparently a woman had called to his house yesterday and she had handed him a parcel. The package contained his old war medals. I was so glad to hear that some good had come out of the conflict we had had with those scumbags. They won't be giving him a hard time anymore.

I could see a vast difference in Carol and Frank that day, they both seemed a lot better in themselves. Carol looked more confident and Frank's old face no longer had that tormented look.

Over a week had passed by since that justifiable incident that we had sorted out on our old council estate. Although I knew it wasn't over, and it never would be, not until I got justice for Carol.

Steve and Carl had arranged another meet with me; it was to be at my apartment. I thought to myself, my pad was starting to be transformed into an office by the looks of things. Although on second thoughts I preferred it that way. Steve had asked me if I would mind if he brought Chris his cousin along. He assured me he was dead sound and of course, also family. Once I knew Chris was blood related, and more so he was Jimmy's nephew, one of my best friends, I agreed.

When Chris was introduced to me he shook my hand firmly. I like that in a person, a good strong handshake to me shows that a person has sincerity. There's nothing more irritating than a person half heartedly giving you a limp hand shake. Looking at Chris was just like looking at Steve, they appeared so alike. In fact, they looked like twins rather than first cousins.

Steve said to me his cousin Chris, who also lived on the estate, wanted to be involved with the three of us. He laid it out to me how Chris was dead game and could really handle himself. He was also very discreet and he would trust him with his life.

'Why?' I asked Chris. 'You haven't even got a blemish on your character. In fact none of you have. I mean if any of us ever come unstuck, and I'm not saying we will but there's always that chance, the consequences could be very severe.'

'I'm willing to take my chances.' Answered Chris. 'Look, I hate those lowlife bastards and what they have been getting up to on our estate, people have had enough of it all. What happened a couple of weeks ago, when you put those three animals in hospital, was just brilliant; and a lot of the neighbours were made up over it by the way. One of the scum is still on the critical list, rumour has it he will end up a cabbage.'

'Ok Chris.' I said. 'I don't mind if you want to team up with us, to be honest, we could do with another pair of hands.'

'Yeah John and I've told our Chris that the *best* way is *your* way. Like you said, we keep going for their top man whatever gang of scum bags we come across.'

Chris went on to explain to me that he worked as a doorman in the clubs and if we ever did need any more hands he knew the right guys.

I got concerned when he told me he could bring in more men to join up with us. I stipulated to him he must never tell anybody who we were and what we got up to. The four of us must keep it close knit at all times. I also told him that the way we work; we just keep doing our own hit and run tactics. We will make it like a sort of S.A.S. unit.

'After all,' I said to them. 'The I.R.A was only a small cell and they were fairly successful in the operations they carried out.'

So this was the way our little posse was formed, nobody else would ever penetrate our circle and so as not to arouse suspicion; during day times we didn't socialise with each other. When we did arrange meets and get-togethers it was imperative that it should always take place at my apartment and never around any council ghettos.

Throughout the forthcoming weeks we started chastising gangs of hooligans who were getting out of order, not only on our old estate but we started stretching out to other areas around and about. We were very active. Always doing it the same way; copping for the hard case out of them and dealing with just him, but most of them were only about fourteen to fifteen years of age. There was one main gang who were slightly older and were bang into vandalising anything they came across. Smashing gravestones up in local cemeteries and causing misery and heartache to local families who had loved ones buried there.

CHASTISING THE GRAVE VANDALS

One day Steve and I were having a stroll around the city centre. We had been hanging around and having a coffee and tea here and there. Whilst we were both having our little mooch, Steve bought the evening newspaper. We both sat down outside some cafe bar and after ordering some drinks Steve started browsing through the paper. 'John have you seen this?'

He showed me a big article on the front page. There was a photograph of a young woman, she was looking very upset in the photograph and was standing by her baby daughter's vandalised grave. Little ornaments and dolls could be seen all broken into bits around the baby's graveside. There was also a photo of local mothers and families outside the cemetery and they were holding up placards protesting for something to be done to stop these senseless acts of vandalism.

When I had finished looking at the front page of the paper Steve said. 'I'm not having that; my grandparents are buried in that cemetery.'

I borrowed the paper from Steve and looked for myself. It was the local cemetery where most of our families are buried. I went on reading; there was an article about the local priest, Father McCarthy, to the local people he was known as 'Father Mac'. It seemed as though, according to the paper, he was begging the local authorities for help. It was believed that these sick hooligans had been intimidating the priest himself. It also appeared that these gangs invaded the cemetery non-stop at weekends. Once again as usual it was the same old story; nothing was being done to prevent these despicable acts.

'Let's get this sorted John,' said Steve angrily. 'We can't sit back and let this happen, I wanna steam in there and batter the lot of those scum bags.'

I totally agreed with him, so we arranged a call out (getting the rest of our circle together). Through the rest of the week we did a bit of research on the cemetery. One of the local neighbours who lived yards away from the cemetery came up with a name for us; Billy Jones, or 'Bone eye Jones' was his nickname. He was the local terror and the main instigator of the rest of the gang. We were informed that each Friday and Saturday night, he and his gang of thugs would come to the cemetery, mostly on their push bikes, bringing with them bottles of beer and wine and go completely off their heads. Then they would kick off with the vandalism, smashing up the graves of people's loved ones.

The local community that lived around there were also going through a bad period. To them, it was like a living a nightmare. I believe some of those local people had tried on numerous occasions to quell it all, but they had been met with intimidation. In some cases they were threatened that their homes would be set on fire. This was all down, of course, to Billy Jones.

We had found out where this young terror lived, and at one point in our plans, we were thinking about snatching him from his house, and taking him away to do the damage on him. We later found out though that he lived with his parents and the rest of his family, so we knocked that idea back and did what we usually did and that was to sit off somewhere inside the cemetery, when the right moment came along, only then would we capture him. The day before the action, Steve and I had visited the cemetery during day and had seen the devastation for ourselves, whilst there we got talking to a couple of guys who were working in the cemetery, they were gravediggers. One of the guys, who looked the oldest out of the two, told us he had never known anything like it the way these young thugs were wrecking the place. He went on to tell us that a few weeks earlier he and his other work mate had just dug two fresh graves for the following day's burials. When they both arrived for work the next morning, both graves had been half filled in with broken gravestones and all kinds of rubbish, beer bottles etc. As if that wasn't bad enough he went on, one of the sick bastards had crapped inside one of the graves.

Steve and I both left the two workers that morning absolutely disgusted. We went over, whilst we were still in the cemetery, to visit Steve's family grave, where thankfully we found it had not been vandalised... as yet!

'Let's hurry up and get these bastards John.'

'No worries mate we might have a bit of luck tonight,' I replied.

That same night, which happened to be a Friday, all four of us were patiently sitting off inside of the cemetery. We had brought with us some good equipment; powerful torches and other bits and bobs. The plan was; when these thugs arrived we would quietly surround them and when we had them placed, on a given signal, we would then shine our torches right on them and after quickly surrounding the scumbags we would then beat them unmercifully with our wooden battens. Once this had been done, my next move would be to get their main man, a Mr Billy 'bone eye' Jones.

I remember that Friday night very vividly. Those vandals did come into the cemetery, and like we'd been told they were all on pushbikes. I remember them peddling around the graves screaming and shouting to each other, there were about five or six in number. I wanted them all off their bikes before we launched our attack.

After a few minutes their erratic behaviour slowed down a bit, they all came to a holt on their bikes, and just as I had wanted they got off and parked them up. Funnily enough it was by a freshly dug empty grave. We could hear them laughing at one another and swigging out of bottles of alcohol. One of them stood over the empty grave and started having a piss in it; another one threw a bottle into it. All this time and unbeknown to them we had been slowly and quietly crawling on our stomachs, surrounding them. We started creeping up nearer and nearer. When I knew we had them in reach I gave the signal to attack. It went down treat. We all got up switching our torches on, and at the same time ran towards them with our baseball bats. Panic set in and one of them screamed.

'It's them vigilantes!'

We laid into them all, battering them to the ground. Within minutes they were all lying smashed to pieces and moans and groans could be heard coming from their broken bodies. Now we had them where we wanted, I said to the lot of them. 'Which one of you is the Billy Jones fella?'

There was a bit of a silence so I grabbed the nearest one to me by his hair, I then smashed my wooden batten right across his mouth. It was a wicked blow. I then went for another one of them and before I raised my batten he pointed Billy Jones out to me. Funnily enough, he was the one we saw pissing in the grave.

I said to him dead coldly, 'I'm gonna make a fuckin' mess of you, you fuckin' prick.'

I looked at him; his condition was already in a bad way. I got Steve to give me a hand with him and we both dragged him to the empty grave, the one he had just soiled. When we had him there I raised the wooden batten, I don't know whether he heard what I said to him but I told him anyway.

'You won't be vandalising anymore graves, you fuckin' scumbag.'

I began smashing in his knees and his arms, and then I gave him the final blow right across his nose. I heard it break. He was out! I turned and said to Steve, 'let's throw him in this open grave and see how he likes it when he wakes up.'

'Yeah,' said Steve. 'I'm all for burying the rat.'

We didn't bury him; instead we threw a couple of their bikes on top of him. 'Let's see how he likes that when he wakes up,' I said to Steve.

It must have been about two o'clock in the morning when we had finished. I turned to Carl. 'Get yourself cleaned up a little bit mate and go and tell the priest what has happened.'

He went and knocked on Father Mac's house, which was adjoining the cemetery. Carl informed the priest where a gang of badly injured young men could be found, believed to be the ones responsible for vandalising the graves. Steve then left our calling card amongst the scum it read: JUSTICE HAS BEEN DONE.

GIVE THEM A MEDAL

Along the way, still carrying on with our cleaning up project, we had been informed about another gang of cowardly scumbags. According to the locals, this gang we were told about were far worse than all the other lot put together.

One night, the said gang had been running havoc and had set two cars on fire, one of the cars belonged to a disabled pensioner who we all knew personally.

A few weeks previously they had broken into her bungalow whilst she slept. They literally dragged the old lady out of bed and after beating her up, ransacked the home and stole her few treasured possessions including her husband's pocket watch and other sentimental belongings. It all left her badly traumatised.

Anyway, a fire engine came on the scene of the two burning cars. The fire crew started tackling the fires, but then the gang turned on the firemen. They started pelting them with bricks, glass bottles and any other sort of missiles they could lay their hands on. The fire crew had to abandon everything due to one of the crew being shot in the face by a pellet gun, as well as some of them being injured by flying debris. All the time this was happening not one police car had turned up…. typical!

Since we had heard of this old lady's terrible ordeal at the hands of this gang, we had had them under observation, of which *they* were completely unaware. We had singled out the main instigator of this lawless marauding gang. This bastard had some time ago, hijacked a car from a woman. The young mother had her baby in the back seat of the car. After dragging and punching the woman to the ground he then drove like a mad man around the estate. He then abandoned the car and the baby outside a block of flats. The woman was traumatised over it all and so was the baby, a four-year-old girl.

On the particular night that *we* were on the scene, we followed them to a busy High Street. Carl and I were sitting off in the van watching their every move, whilst Steve and Chris where walking about on foot. The prick had a pellet gun on him and started shooting at any passing cars or buses that were driving along the main street. The thing is, as I've said before, it's pointless for us to steam in on them because it would just end up in a pitch battle, then most probably a mad scattering match afterwards. No, that wasn't the way to go about it; putting ourselves on offer and getting identified. So although anger was building up inside me at what this bastard was up to tonight, we just had to wait and bide our time. I knew the gang would be splitting up at the end of the night and making their way home, some going in separate directions. So we waited and waited.

When they eventually tired of their dangerous pastime, they *did* disband, and we followed the vile ringleader. We kept on his tail till the time was right, and then we got him. We took him down to the docks, the place we had him was nice and secluded, it was also pitch black down there.

Chris and I held him by his ankles and we dangled him over the edge of a wall. On the other side of it was the River Mersey, and it was a very long drop below. I threatened to throw him in and he started crying uncontrollably. We finally dragged him back up. He was whimpering on the floor completely freaked out. I bent down and told him that if he and his gang of scumbags didn't stop their antics we were coming back just for him. I went to the van and got the pellet gun that I had taken off him earlier, together with the lead pellets he had in a small tin. I told Steve and the others what I intended to do with this scumbag, I said I was going to pepper him all over with these lead pellets.

'Don't worry,' I assured them. 'I won't kill him'

Steve and Chris stood on his out stretched arms and I jammed one of his socks into his mouth, I noticed he had sticking out ears so I just put the nozzle of the gun close to each ear and kept shooting. I kept reloading it, I must have put about ten fuckin' lead pellets in each ear, I then shot a few into the back of his hands. After I had finished shooting at him, I pulled the sock away from his mouth and I looked down at him. Feeling no remorse for what I had just done to him I then proceeded to smash in his nose and mouth with the butt of the gun; I was beginning to get carried away. Carl had to stop me from going too far. The hatred I had for those scumbags was starting to go beyond my control. I threw the pellet gun into the River Mersey and the four of us just looked down on the whimpering rat.

'What's the next move John?' Steve asked. 'Are we dropping him off anywhere?'

'No.' I said, 'We will leave him here. Let the prick crawl home for all I care.'

It was splashed all over the newspaper the next day:

'A seventeen year-old youth was abducted by a gang of masked men. He was found badly injured and had been shot several times all over his body. It is believed he is well known to the police and he comes from the same notorious Wood Green council estate. The police report said 'It is the same gang of men who are responsible for several other attacks on youths in the area.'

The violence we had been inflicting on the street gangs had started to draw attention from the press and media. They wanted to know more about the masked vigilante gang who were said to be responsible. On one page of a certain newspaper an injured fireman could be seen lying in a hospital bed. It went on to tell how he had lost the sight in one eye. It appeared that he and his crewmates were the ones we had heard about, that were trying to put out the car fires on the Wood Green estate and had come under attack by the gang of thugs we had dealt with. The newspaper described in detail what had gone on. It went on to say that one of the gang was firing an air pistol at the fire crew, hence the loss of a man's eye. A news journalist in an interview with the injured fireman asked him what his thoughts where about the masked vigilante gang? He was quoted as saying: 'they should be given a medal'.

Almost Exposed

Now that the press had started to highlight the stories about the turmoil and the goings on, on this notorious estate, it had brought about a strong police presence. It's a shame it had to take something like this to bring a police force out. They should have been patrolling the streets in the first place. With the estate getting all this attention, I suggested to our circle that we should cease all our activities immediately, at least until things had died down a bit. I explained to them it would be too dangerous to continue, so we all decided to keep a low profile. It would only be on a temporarily basis, after all we had sorted a few of the scumbags out and had cleaned the streets up a bit.

A week had passed by since all the commotion that had been going on. Steve and I had been in constant touch by phone. He told me that Carl had been monitoring the bizzies every move. At first the bizzies where crawling all over the place, he had told us, but now it had been whittled down, except for the odd one or two police cars that had been patrolling around.

When I had heard that the dust had settled down a bit, I thought now is as good a time as any to pay old Frank and Carol a visit. I hadn't seen them for over two weeks although we had kept in touch by phoning each other. The next morning I got in to my car and drove the five miles or so to the Wood Green estate. I stopped at Carol's first and we spent a good hour together, talking our heads off. She even laughed a few times which was a good sign. Carol's house was now fully secured and I could see she felt a lot safer.

After I had seen her that morning and before I arrived at old Frank's house I pulled up outside the local newsagents and off licence. I walked into the shop and saw a few yobs where messing about inside. They all stopped what they were doing when they saw me come in. Then they all walked out of the place. I thought to myself, that's a bit strange, but just shrugged it off. I asked the shop assistant for a packet of pipe tobacco and a small bottle of brandy, which was obviously for old Frank. When I went to pay for the goods the man and woman who I had recognised previously from the last time I was in there, refused to take my money. Puzzled, I asked them why? They were both smiling at me friendly like, the woman sort of waved her arms and told me to keep them. I insisted that I pay but she point blank refused,

'You good man,' she said in broken English.

What could I do? They both introduced themselves to me; their name was Khan, Mr and Mrs Khan. I had a little chat with them and they seemed very nice people. We were talking away when the conversation suddenly changed; they started telling me about all the turmoil that had been going on in and around the estate. It was quite obvious that these two hard-working people had been living under a lot of stress. This was all down, of course, to the unruly behaviour of the lowlife yobs. They went on to tell me they had a fourteen year old son named Amir, but that he couldn't hang about outside because he was forever getting all kinds of verbal and intimidating abuse from the bullying yobs.

Somehow I had a feeling that these two people had tumbled to who I was. I don't know how, but I was starting to get a feeling that my cover might have been blown here. It all seemed too much of a coincidence, what with those kids and the reaction from them when I entered the shop. I had the same sort of treatment half an hour later when I was visiting old Frank. Whilst I was in Frank's he had started to tell me about the rowdy neighbours who lived next door to him. It appeared that on more than one occasion, they had been calling on Frank and asking him if he was alright and whether he needed any errands running or anything. I thought to myself that was a turn about coming from them. Instead of being so inconsiderate to him they were now starting to show some respect for a change. It does only prove one thing though; they had to be threatened by us before some order was restored.

When I was leaving Frank's house those same neighbours also showed out to me. They said hello and how was I doing? Which was sort of all dead friendly like. Now all of this nice friendly behaviour, especially coming from these sorts of people, really convinced me that they all thought I was definitely involved with the violence which had been getting dished out on the lowlife. They all may have thought that it was me, but that meant nothing, proving it was something else. That is why I had to be so vigilant and not make any mistakes, there-by getting myself arrested.

Blunders Exposed

These days any sort of incriminating evidence the police have got against you must be absolutely paramount. They cannot afford to make any slip-ups what so ever, otherwise a clever lawyer representing the defendant could find a loophole, or for a better word, a flaw in the case. This is happening in courtrooms more frequently now than ever before. Mostly because of crown prosecutors and police blunders being made. Usually when this does happen there is a public outcry. People voice their opinion of utter disgust over it all, and who can blame them? It would be more of an outrage to the public if the person that was standing trial was exposed as a lowlife mugger or a child molester, and because of these blunders these animals are allowed to walk free from court. As has happened on some occasions. The judge, who has presided over one of these messed up cases, usually reprimands the police and the crown prosecutor for these grave errors they have made. But then, let's not forget the cost of the time wasted and trial, plus the taxpayer's money.

However, there is another side to the coin; what about the judge himself? He is not all that infallible; he too can make a botch up. Oh yes, that can happen, in fact it is becoming more frequent than one would think. Try and comprehend this; let's say a lowlife predator has unanimously been found guilty of a heinous crime. The judge is entitled to use his own discretion on how to establish imposing a sentence, which by the way is usually lenient these days compared to what it should be for one of these animals. When he, the judge, is addressing the jury in his summing up, sometimes he can make a grave mistake; by being biased towards the defendant, or some other important issue. A clever lawyer who is defending can pick up on this and could have a strong point of law for an appeal. The appellant is usually successful meaning the lowlife scumbag is set free. When this does happens it is then the judge's turn to be ridiculed. Not only by the police as one would think, but by the press and the media. No wonder the public are in an uproar when a catastrophe like this happens. I myself have witnessed families and mothers protesting vigorously for justice. Like I have mentioned before, we in this country of England are led to believe we have the best and fairest law in the world. I suppose we have, that is, if it is practiced right. Law and order is essential to our society, we have to have it, if we didn't, our mothers, sisters and children would not be safe to walk in the street. Not that the streets are safe these days or anywhere else for that matter. So is it any wonder some people take the law into their own hands when they have been denied justice.

THE BEAST

This brings me on to the next objective; it is about some filthy evil beast my friends and I had hunted down. It all started when a friend of a friend who was asking us for our help had approached Steve and me. Some woman's ten-year-old daughter had been brutally raped. Now if we were to capture this animal I knew I would be putting him in a really bad way. So I didn't want to put myself and the rest of our circle on offer; meaning us being identified. This then put us all in an awkward position because none of us could afford to see the woman to get the full score from her. It was then decided that Carl, who had a friend that knew the woman personally would be doing the negotiating with the mother. The information about the paedophile would be relayed back to our unit.

To begin with, we were told the paedophile had at first started grooming the girl, it then led on to him intimidating her with all kinds of threats, just so he could have his own way with her. According to a psychiatrist's medical report; which had been read out to the court, the beast had done the most unimaginable filth to the child, which is too sickening to describe. She was now under constant medication and not only was her little body ruined but her young mind was completely messed up too. This animal was about to stand trial for rape, but the evidence against him was very weak. He had been very clever, like most paedophiles are, whilst carrying out these monstrous acts. He had left no traces of D.N.A. the only evidence the police had against him was the little girls statement, but would that stand up in court? Would it fuck! This animal was going to walk free from court and escape justice... or so he thought.

I ask Carl, 'What about the girl's father? Why hasn't he done something about this? I mean if it was my child I would not hesitate, I wouldn't think twice about the consequences. I would just kill the bastard there and then even if it meant me doing a life sentence.'

After I had calmed down a bit, Carl said to me, 'John he *is* the girl's father, well her step father; her *real* dad is dead.'

Well that says it all doesn't it? Don't get me wrong I'm not saying all stepfathers are paedophiles. There are some decent men who have and do take on somebody else's kids. I suppose what is the hardest part for a woman is finding the right man they can trust. Some women can be so gullible when it comes to being charmed by a very persuasive so-called gentleman. Paedophiles are masters at that game. Here we have a decent lady, with a little daughter, she has lost her husband, time has dragged on a bit and she has become very lonely and insecure. What does she do? She goes and advertises in a lonely-hearts column for some male company. In her advert she explains in all innocence something about her background for example, she is a widow with a lovely little daughter. Reading an advert like that is a paedophile's dream, a great opportunity for the sick bastard. That is what happened here, she met who she thought was a nice, charming gentleman and married him, but underneath this entire masquerade was a filthy predator who preyed on this woman's vulnerability.

Whilst his trial was taking place Steve and I had been sitting in court watching and listening to the evidence the police had against him. As we were listening to most of it and by the way the trial was being conducted, I knew there and then, there just wasn't enough concrete evidence to convict. The beast himself knew this too. It made me sick to watch him sitting there in the dock with his suit on and all smarmy looking. Just because of some legal argument that his lawyer had come up with, the judge directed the jury to acquit on the grounds of insufficient evidence, just like I had predicted. He was found not guilty. He walked out of that courtroom smiling and proclaiming to some waiting press reporters, how innocent he was.

After the paedophile's trial and a few weeks had passed by, we had done all our homework on that beast. It was now time for the unit and I to put things into action. We already knew where he lived, he had moved into some rented accommodation. A house just by; believe it or not, a kids school. I had done a stake out on his house quite a few times, watching his comings and goings. Nobody in the neighbourhood knew his identification as that was kept a secret by the ridiculous laws, which have by the way, recently been enforced just to protect the likes of that filthy beast.

The night before we went to capture him, I decided the four of us should stay in my apartment and that we should move out first thing in the morning, which would be a Monday. By doing it this way we wouldn't arouse any suspicion on ourselves. It was still fairly dark at six o'clock in the morning, plus there was less activity on the roads. We had already parked our van in the area the night before; it had all the equipment we would be using locked up inside it. Just before we had left my apartment that Monday morning I went over everything with a fine toothcomb, with Steve, Carl and Chris. To be honest I started to get a buzz out of all the planning and organising I was conducting with these three young men.

I started to feel it was taking me back to when my friends and I were bang at it years before. We would all be geared up and our adrenaline would be pumping away getting ready to pull off a good robbery, such as burning through a safe in the volt of some bank. The graft we were doing was very heavy most of the time, and if it was successful, afterwards we would all be sitting around a table in some safe house sharing out the spoils. That's when the buzz really kicked in for us.

This time however, what I am about to embark on is different all together, I felt as though my mind was starting to get carried away with the terrible beatings I was giving to these lowlife scum bags. I don't know why, but each time I captured one of these animals, I showed them no mercy what so ever. The violence I inflicted upon them was becoming more and more brutal. Maybe it was affecting me this way because each time we captured one of these animals; they seemed to be more evil than the last one.

Anyway, back to our strategy; to begin with Carl was going to do the fronting up. He would be dressed up as policeman and ring the paedophile's doorbell. Hopefully he would open it, but really, there would be no problem not when he saw a uniformed policeman standing there. Carl had played the part absolutely brilliantly that morning. I still remember what he said to that paedophile when the front door had been opened.

'Sorry to bother you first thing in the morning sir, can I have a word? The station has sent me around?'

'You most certainly can officer,' answered the paedo.' 'Do come in.'

I had instructed Carl beforehand that the minute he gained access Steve and I would be no more than thirty seconds behind him. I also instructed Chris that once we were inside he was to bring the van around and to back it right up the pathway to the front door of the house. Everything went according to plan. Steve had gone straight up the stairs to make sure no one else was in there. The beast was sitting down with a dressing gown on holding his two hands to his face and shaking.

'Could you please tell me what all this is about? I have done nothing wrong.'

I put my masked face up to him. My appearance alone must have terrified him. I spoke to him in a low menacing voice.

'You what? You've done nothing wrong? You filthy lowlife scum. You've got a short memory haven't you? You raped a little girl!'

He moaned back to me. 'She wasn't a little girl, she was ten. I didn't do it.'

I couldn't believe what I was hearing from this paedophile and this only infuriated me more.

'The judge found me not guilty,' he went on protesting.

'Oh, I know he did,' I said to him sarcastically. 'But he wasn't a real judge now was he? I am the judge now, and do you know what? I have just found you guilty, you filthy beast.'

I had brought a pair of handcuffs with me and some tape. We proceeded to handcuff him and tape his mouth up. Steve who had been looking around upstairs had come back down carrying a cardboard box.

'Look at this! It's full of child porn, that dirty fucker is still at it.'

I told Steve to leave it all in there, but then I changed my mind and we put some of the photographs in the pockets of his dressing gown.

'Let the bizzies find all this.' I said.

We quickly bundled him into the back of the van and drove towards the school, which was only about thirty yards down the road.

The gates were open when we got there and it was still fairly dark. Chris drove the van inside the school grounds pulling up a little out of view from the main road. We then dragged the animal out of the van, I told Steve not to damage his face or head, just to break every limb in his body. We began beating him unmercifully with wooden pickaxe handles, his body was a heap on the floor when we had finished, and it was completely broken.

I though took the punishment a step further, I went to the van and pulled out our tool bag, and from it I took out an old blowtorch. I lit it and then I proceeded to burn his dick off and the rest of his anatomy underneath. Carl and Chris turned away, but I couldn't control myself. I thought about what this beast had done to that baby girl. Who knows, it's possible he might have done it to other kids in the past. This then drove me on to mutilate him more. Carl came over to me with his hand clasped to his mouth. I will admit it was all getting a bit messy. 'John, John!' He said, 'Stop it that's enough.'

He tried to pull me away. I stopped what I was doing and stood up. The animal was completely ruined. I thought, 'Fuck him! He won't be raping any more babies ever again'. I walked away from the heap of mess on the floor and I beckoned Carl over to me.

'Never, ever, interfere with the punishment I am giving to these beasts.' I told him. 'That is the second time you have gone against the grain with me, and you went and shouted my name!'

Steve interrupted. 'There are no worries about that John he's well out of it. He wouldn't even know what day it was; never mind about your name.'

I looked at Carl and told him that if he didn't like the way I perform he could walk away for all I care. I also said to him, 'don't you realise

136

that we are dealing with the lowest form of human beings here?'

He then meekly apologised, to me. He told me it was making him sick from the smell and everything else.

'Ok, let's forget about it all.' I said to him.

The next move I had planned was to handcuff the paedophile to the school gates. I thought it would be an appropriate way to expose this animal, on full view. This we did, and to finish off, Steve had brought a big placard from the van that we had already made, we hung it around his neck. It read:

THIS BEAST RAPES LITTLE GIRLS. JUSTICE HAS BEEN DONE.

It didn't look a pretty sight!

After leaving that horrible mess at the school gates. We drove the van to where Steve's car was parked ready for the switch over. I told Steve and the rest of the team that I would be getting shut of the van today. We had had it a bit too long, and who knows, it could well have been identified. I also insisted that they leave all their masks and gloves in the van with me, I would destroy them as-soon-as too.

From start to finish, the whole operation we had just done that morning took less than twenty minutes. Steve got into his car with Carl and Chris as I drove away in the van.

The next day as I expected, the whole of the city was confronted with the news about yesterday's events, regarding the kidnap and torture of a paedophile. Some news had gone nationwide, even as far as getting reports on television bulletins. It was reported that a man who had been recently charged with child rape had been found badly mutilated, and that the police are now convinced it is the same gang of vigilantes who are responsible for other similar attacks in and around the city.

A BOSS CHRISTMAS

For myself, Steve and the rest of the unit, it was another case of keeping our heads down for a while. My two brothers had come to visit me, Christmas was almost on top of us and I was invited to a Christmas bash they were having together with Jimmy and Paul. They had booked some classy restaurant in the city and then it was back to one of their houses for a party. It could not have come at a better time for me; I could do with chilling out for a while, so I was definitely up for it. This would be the first Christmas I would have had at home for almost six years. I can't believe how time passes so quickly. I almost forgot that before going to the party I had to see old Frank and Carol, being Christmas time and everything.

So the next day I made my way up to visit Frank and Carol. I gave Frank a little prezzie and spent a bit of time with him, he was over the moon with it all. I then called at Carol's; I had a surprise for her too. When she opened her front door to me I passed her a cardboard box with a red Christmas ribbon tied around it. She opened it up when we were inside her house. I was watching Carol's face when she opened up the box, and out popped the head of a little brown and white Jack Russell puppy. Carol was really thrilled and she looked at me excitedly.

'What shall I call him?'

'It's not a *he*, it's a *she*…. you know a little girl dog?' I laughed

'Oh!' she said, still excited. 'I didn't realise.'

It was good to see Carol like her old self again. I handed her a card and a bottle of Moet champagne.

'Oh, John thanks!' She then threw her arms around me and gave me a kiss.

I told her not to open the Moet until Christmas and said that I would share a glass with her.

'Honest John?' she asked. 'Will you come and see me at Christmas?'

'Yeah, I'll be here,' I told her.

'Promise me?' She said.

'I promise.' I replied.

As I got up to leave, Carol stood up holding the little pup.

'What name shall I give her?' She asked me.

I shrugged and thought for a moment.

'How about Kate or Katie? Yeah, Katie is a nice little name for a girl dog, what do you think?'

We both burst out laughing. Then I left. As I drove away from Carols I still had that burning desire to capture that lowlife animal that had caused her all that pain and suffering she had been through. I knew I would get him in the end, it was only a matter of time, and when I did it would be..... God help him!

The Christmas party my brothers and friends had arranged for me was fairly impressive, with all the trimming and everything, but to be honest I felt as though something was missing. Maybe I was just feeling a bit sorry for myself. After all Christmases are for families and loved ones. As usual Jimmy was the life and soul of the party displaying all his antics and joking around with everybody. He introduced me to some woman who was a friend of his wife's.

'John this is Joan, she has been dying to meet you.' He said laughing.

Joan was a fairly attractive woman who looked in her thirties, she was ok I suppose, we had a drink and we were both having a good chat and everything, but then after a while, she got really blitzed and started talking a load of rubbish to me. She started name dropping about people she knew and asked me if I knew any of them? I don't like this sort of talk. I started to blank her, then she got a bit out of hand so I decided to 'do one.' I didn't say goodbye to her or anyone else at the party. I just sort of sloped away unnoticed. It's funny when you meet a person and they're sober they seem as good as gold, but if that person has got a problem with the bottle you can get such a shock. Their whole character can change like *Jekyll and Hyde*.

I ended up phoning Carol. It was Christmas Eve, so I told her to open that bottle of Moet as I was on my way up to hers. I wasn't going to Carol's to try to rekindle anything from the past, it's just that she was good company and we could both relate to each other. After all we were both approaching fifty and, although our youth and looks had passed us by, our minds were still young at heart really. Do you know what? It was one of the best Christmases I had had in years. We both sat there drinking and having a laugh. She played some old soul music for me, and it really chilled me right out. Soul music is my favourite, especially when a black girl or a black man sings it with the beautiful voices that they have been gifted with. Yeah, Carol and I had a boss Christmas together. When it was all over I started thinking to myself.... I wonder what the New Year is going to bring.

HUNTING A SERIAL MUGGER

The Beginning of January 2006

My friends and I were informed about a ruthless mugger, who operated in and around our old estate preying on vulnerable pensioners. Now I'm not talking about a kid here, this person we were after was in his late thirties. This animal didn't care if some of the old people he mugged were disabled or even blind. His method was lying in wait like an ambusher, mostly around post offices on pension days and payouts.

This lowlife I am describing was a real evil bastard to most of his victims. We were told that sometimes if he failed to get any money from the old people, he would then resort to the callous method he was noted for. He would pull the rings from women's fingers, always after he had beaten them up. On some of these occasions if he couldn't extract their rings easily he would literally suck their fingers to get the rings off, sometimes he went as far as breaking their fingers. Over the past twelve months these vicious muggings had been highlighted in the local newspapers and photographs showed the most appalling injuries these old people had suffered. One photo that really got to me was of an old retired nurse showing her poor old face with black eyes and fractured cheekbones. This was all because that animal had had a hard time trying to wrench the little gold wedding ring from her frail finger.

As far as myself and my friends were concerned, this lowlife had to be sorted out fast. But first as always, we had to plan how to go about capturing this evil predator. We had to be extra vigilant on this one not to put ourselves in any sort of jeopardy, from now on things had to be done meticulously, which gave me an idea.

Years before when I was grafting with my friends from the old school Jimmy, Paul and my brother Vincent, we were doing some heavy graft at that time and this particular move was a bank we were about to rob. I was disguised as an old invalid in a wheelchair. Paul was pushing me inside the premises and I had a sawn off shotgun hidden underneath the blanket that was across my knees. The shotgun I had was used as a frightener, Jimmy and Vincent where already inside the premises; they were both dressed in suits and ties like businessmen.

The plan was; I would be pushed up to the counter where the big stash of readies where bagged (incidentally, before we went on this move we had been informed by a reliable source where the money would be). Doing that move went off just perfect for us that day and it went something like this,

The crippled invalid in the wheelchair suddenly stood up and sprang into action covering everybody in there with the weapon he had had concealed. The rest of our team knew exactly what to do. Paul went over the top grill of the bank counter like a cat, then he quickly passed the bags of readies to Vincent. In less than two minutes; and that was all it took, we were out of there and gone with the prize. Little did I realise I would be doing that same sort of move years later. The only difference this time was I was not going after a large amount of money, instead I was going after a lowlife scum bag who I would make a mess of, and do you know what? I'm not even getting a penny for doing it.

I often thought to myself 'here I am sticking my neck out and putting myself on the line. I mean, if I was caught doing one of these violent acts and sentenced in a court of law, I know I would not see daylight again'. So what was it that drove me on? So often I began to think; 'am I starting to lose it or what?' I know it's impossible, but my main objective was to try and get rid of as many lowlife scumbags as I could!

Well here I am, sitting in a wheelchair dressed up to look like an old man. It was a cold winter's day, late in the afternoon. Carl who was wearing glasses and a woolly hat pulled over his head was pushing me in the wheelchair. I turned and said to him, 'it's a good job I have this blanket wrapped around my knee's I'm freezing sitting here in this chair.'

Carl was looking down and he started laughing at me. Now up until then I hadn't know Carl had a sense of humour, he always seemed sort of serious in his mannerisms. He jokingly said to me (which came as a surprise), 'oh shut up grandad, and stop your moaning, I'll soon be putting you to bed with your hot water bottle tucked in?'

Then he burst out laughing his head off. We both looked at one another for a second then he started laughing again and that kicked me off too, we were both nearly pissing ourselves.

Anyway, back to business, Steve and Chris were sitting off and waiting in the different van we had acquired. The four of us had been going over our strategy and now was the time to act. Carl knew this mugger by sight through a bit of homework he had been doing on him. We had also, through another source, managed to get word back to the scumbag that an old pensioner in a wheelchair would be drawing out of the Post Office a large amount of his savings, at about half past four that afternoon. If and when we captured this animal we had the ideal place to take him to.

It was now twenty minutes past four and it was going dark being that it was mid-wintertime. My mobile rang. It was Steve.

'Ok John?' he said. 'Any signs of the prick?'

Steve could plainly see Carl and I from where he was parked. 'Not yet,' I told him, 'but we are about to go over to the post office now.'

The post office was just across the street; Carl had just started to push me across when all of a sudden he got excited. 'John, there's that bastard on the corner, but he has another scumbag with him.'

'Don't worry about the other one.' I told him. 'We'll get that sorted, just get me inside the post office.'

Carl pushed me into the premises, he told me the mugger was still waiting on the corner and was watching us both go in. I told Carl to phone Steve straight away and tell him to get ready and be on standby for when we came out. Carl then told me the mugger had seen us and was looking through the window of the post office. This was all going according to plan; in fact it was better, because they had fallen for the decoy. I pulled out a cloth bank bag when it was my turn to be served at the counter, I passed it to the assistant, it was full of thirty pounds worth of coins. I asked if I could change it into notes, I now knew that the animal outside with his accomplice was watching me through that window, being convinced I was coming out of this post office with a little stash.

When we both came out of the post office it was a lot darker, which for us was brilliant, but we couldn't see the muggers. Carl started pushing me along the street then he said,

'There they are, we're just about to pass them.'

The pair of scumbags had been waiting in the doorway of a closed shop, which was at the end of the block. When we passed them Carl said in a low voice, 'they are on our tail John, they are just a few yards behind us.'

'That's ok,' I said quietly. 'Head towards Steve and Chris in the van.'

I then chuckled to Carl. 'We are about to be mugged. Get ready!'

We could hear the footsteps behind us getting closer and closer. Suddenly, the two predators had both pulled their hoods up and had caught up with us positioning themselves at either side of the wheelchair. They started walking at our slow pace and then one of them quickly skipped a couple of paces in front of the wheelchair, making us stop. Steve and Chris were still in the van only a few metres away. The one who made the wheelchair stop spoke to me in a typical scallie accent. 'Give us yeah fuckin' money or I'll smash you and that fuckin' wheelchair up.' He leaned down to my face snarling.

'Come on,' he said. 'Give us yeah fuckin' money grandad, we know that you just got your pension. Are yeah gonna pass it over or what? Come on' 'hurry up or I'll fuckin' batter yeah?'

The other hooded lowlife was sort of dancing about nervously and looking around. I sprang right into action and I butted the animal full force in the face. Getting up out of the chair with the wooden baton I had been holding under the blanket, I whacked him across his jaw and he went down like a sack of potatoes. The other scumbag had shot away like a streak of lightening; he was running like a rabbit out of sight. Steve and Chris had got out of the van within seconds.

I quickly asked Carl,
'Is this the right one I've got here or what?'

Carl nodded. 'Yeah that's him, that's him I recognise him.'

We then quickly over powered him and threw him in the van. Steve was dead calm and started folding the wheelchair up, he put it in the van, me and Carl both bungled ourselves in the back of it then we drove away. Our destination was an old boarded up house, Steve through knowing somebody, had somehow acquired the door keys for the premises. We eventually got the mugger inside the place, and sat him down in the middle of the floor. He started trembling, and was holding the injured side of his face. I looked down at him, he was like a cornered rat, I snarled at him. 'So you're the animal who robs and beats up old pensioners are you, you scumbag?'

'No, no, not me, you've got me all wrong.'

'Oh no I haven't. Don't be coming that game with me you fuckin' scumbag.'

I told him the same as I had told the other lowlifes whom I had damaged. 'Listen carefully to what I am going to say; we know everything about you, where you live and who you hang out with. Remember this, you don't know who we are and you never will. You won't be beating and mugging anymore pensioners you fuckin' animal.'

He started whimpering back to me. Trying to sound remorseful. 'I'm sorry, honest to God, honest to God. I won't do it again mate.'

'Oh I know you won't be doing it again,' I told him, 'and another thing, those scum bag mates of yours; you get word to them that we are coming after them too. Right now you're going to get taught a lesson you are never going to forget.'

He started to shiver with fear as I said to him, 'you know what it's like to be terrified now, don't yeah? Like those old people felt when they were at your mercy!'

Before I taped him up I asked him to write his name down on a piece of paper he did so using his right hand. Steve and the rest of our circle all looked at me a quizzically as I asked him to do this.

We kicked off with the punishment on the scumbag. He got the same treatment as the rest of the lowlife got before him. The blows came reigning down on him from our wooden batons. After we had finished he was completely out of it and knocked unconscious. He was lying there on his back both of his arms where out stretched Steve, Carl and Chris thought that was the end of it…. but not me, in fact the punishment wasn't enough as far as I was concerned.

Unbeknown to them I had a sharp meat cleaver in the inside of my jacket. I stood on one of the scumbag's wrists and quickly pulled out the meat cleaver. Carl could see what was about to happen and quickly started to protest. 'No, No! What the fuck are you doing?'

Steve and Chris just stood there in silence. I had selected the right hand of the animal, the hand that had caused all that suffering to those old people. I brought the meat cleaver down onto it with full force. Four of his fingers were severed right off. Carl started to borg as if he was going to vomit at the sight of it all. He then shouted to me.

'Fuck this, there was no need for that, you've chopped his hand off for fucks sake!'

A bit of an argument started to develop between Carl and me. Steve came over and stood between the two of us, he told Carl to take it easy and to calm down. He then pointed to the lowlife on the floor asked me,

'Ok John? What about him, is he staying or going?'

I told him to leave him there and that we should get off. We would phone an ambulance and let them deal with it. Then we drove away from the place in silence. I sensed a gloomy atmosphere. It was quite obvious Carl was dead against what I had just done. I thought to myself, there was only one thing for this... Carl would have to leave our circle; I couldn't work with a guy who was not with me one hundred percent. Just before we had all split we had arranged a meeting the next evening at Chris's place.

THE MEETING AT CHRIS' HOUSE

I was the last one to arrive at Chris's house on the night of the meeting. I had deliberately made myself late for a reason; firstly, I was making sure none of us were under any police surveillance. Secondly, I had sat off Chris's house well before Steve and Carl had got there. I saw them go into the house and when I knew they hadn't been followed I then drove a few times around the neighbourhood. After doing this rec and only when I was fully convinced we were not in any jeopardy, I phoned Chris to tell him I would be there in a couple of minutes. He told me on the phone to hurry as it was all over the news on the television; he said he would leave the door open for me. I did read a couple of the papers that morning, and highlighted were last night's events about the mugger and his injuries. When I got inside Chris's house everybody was sitting glued to the television, it was showing a news update, which was, in my opinion, greatly exaggerated. It described how a man had been found with his hand severed off. His hand hadn't been cut off; we all knew that. This was typical of most journalists; they always seemed to magnify things before the truth finally came out. The television we were all watching started showing the police giving a statement it then showed people from local communities being interviewed by reporters and giving their versions of the previous night's events. The injured serial mugger was known for his vile deeds around there and most of the community were supporting the vigilantes and praising their methods. In another part of the news there was a Muslim businessman who was in total agreement with regards the action taken by the vigilantes. This gentleman said that in his opinion the serial mugger had received the right punishment. The report went on to say that the VIGILANTES were having a strong impact and the police were in an uproar over it all.

When the news program had ended, Carl got up from the chair he had been sitting in; he looked agitated and started to pace up and down. I asked him to get it all off his chest and that if he was not up for any of this business he could call it a day.

'John,' he said to me. 'I think it's all gone a bit too far now, I've had enough of this. I mean, chopping his fuckin' hand off, it made me physically sick.'

'Carl, it was his fingers not his hand.' I reminded him.

'Well anyway,' he went on, 'I want out of this, it's going to bring it all on top for us, we will all be getting nicked next time.'

I looked at Steve and Chris and I could tell that they both felt embarrassed at the way Carl was carrying on. I let Carl go on a bit longer with all his ranting then I stopped him.

'Carl,' I said. 'You know you really surprise me. I didn't know you where so emotional; you're feeling sorry for that scumbag. I would have thought that what your poor old grandmother had to endure when she got violently mugged would have been more upsetting for you than the punishment I had inflicted on that animal. When you and I first met, you did tell me that your old grandmother was brutally mugged, didn't you?'

Carl bowed his head embarrassed. Steve and Chris also looked a little sheepish. Then Carl said to me.

'I understand what you are saying John, but mate, let's face it when it comes to dishing out the violence, you are fuckin' mad! You've got me terrified, you're so unpredictable I don't know what's coming next.'

I listened to him getting it all off his chest. He carried on talking to me,

'John, you can't put the world right. This is happening everywhere, not just here. The police are patrolling our estate now. Old people feel a lot safer. As far as I'm concerned we have done our job, haven't we? I'm all for letting the bizzies take over from now on.'

When Carl had finished what he had to say, I paused for a while then I said to them all,

'Alright, if that's the way you feel Carl, and you; Steve and Chris, I will go along with that, but remember this. The bizzies wont patrol this place for long. You all know what the police are like? Once the dust has settled, they will fuck off like they always do. Let's not forget the other side of the city; those low lives are still at it – muggings and rapes. You never hear of the police presence there – and do you know why? Because no one will stand up to those scum bags – it's completely lawless over there. Can't you see the police are not just there on our estate to protect the old people? The reason they are there is to try and catch us lot, the vigilante gang.'

Steve interrupted.

'John is dead right. What about all those do-gooder's who have been screaming their heads off to the media about how terrible it all is – all those young men being beaten up by vigilantes. It's all one big joke…'please don't hurt our violent muggers!' they might as well be saying.   It's the low-life who are getting protected by the police not the old aged pensioners.'

I went on to tell Carl, Steve and Chris that if they wanted to wrap it all up and get out of it,

156

it was fine by me, but I had one last thing to do before I was finished and that was to hunt down the animal that brutalised Carol. Steve and Chris wouldn't hear of splitting our team up, they both wanted to carry on. However as far as Carl goes? Well he was just sat there with his head bowed when I left Chris's house that night.

At this point in my story I'm beginning to feel I am at a cross roads particularly with Carl who is constantly interrupting me when I'm chastising those scum bags. Ok some of the violence I gave out was brutal, that I'm not denying, but what other alternative did I have? Should I reduce it to a couple of black eyes here and there? Or maybe a broken rib or two? Would that be sufficient enough to deter that lowlife? I don't think so! Another thing that pissed me off, Carl kept repeating to me that I would end up killing one of those animals. All I can say about that is, he had completely underestimated me. I was not that foolish to stick my neck out and commit a murder. I knew how far to go and when to stop. So providing I didn't over step the mark, I would continue maiming those degenerates. I would leave them with scars, scars they would see every day of their lives and never forget as to why they had got them. I really thought Carl's bottle was starting to carry, and that to me had all the hallmarks of a weak link. He could become a danger to the rest of us, I was starting to wonder what the outcome would be if he was arrested and confronted with a strong grilling from the bizzies? Who knows, he could roll over. As from now I thought it would be wrong for me to continue operating with Carl. For that reason, plus other things, I decided the best way forward was for me to go it alone. I was confident I had the ability to sort out what was left of this filthy business. I phoned Steve asking him to meet me and to bring Chris along with him. I needed to explain to the both of them what I was intending to do.

When Steve returned my call he seemed very agitated.

'Haven't you heard the morning news?' He shouted down the phone. 'It's all over the TV'

He went on to tell me that a sex-beast had been found tied to a lamppost at the other side of the city and had been beaten to death. It appears that the murdered paedophile, according to the media, was a known child molester. The police were keeping an open mind and were strongly insinuating it was the same vigilante gang they believed were the ones responsible. Well that's all we needed, didn't we? Some other crew had gone and killed a sex beast and the bizzies were now putting it down to our lot.

Throughout the rest of that week the newspapers and TV bulletins were highlighting more than ever, any stories about the vigilante gang. The police were in an uproar and were appealing for witnesses, stating that somebody most know who this masked gang of murderers were.

I met up with Steve and Chris and after I had explained everything to them Steve was dead cool about it all, and so too was Chris. Both of them were still very game and loyal, but what surprised me more, was when Steve told me that Carl still wanted to be involved. Throughout my life I have always gone with my strong intuition, so I told them both, we will leave Carl out of it for now. The three of us then decided we should all keep away from each other for a few weeks, just to see how it goes.

The very next day my two brothers together with Jimmy and Paul came to my apartment. The four of them seemed very concerned and dead serious looking. I supposed they felt and looked this way because of what had happened, regarding the murder of a paedophile and the police hunting a vigilante gang. I set about fully explaining to them that the killing definitely wasn't down to me or any of our crew. It was only after I had fully explained it all to them that they were convinced. They knew I would never lie to them. We went on to talk about the events for quite some time and we all came to the same conclusion.... it had to be a copycat gang. Afterwards, when our meeting was coming to an end Jimmy said to me.

'We all know you won't stop until you get justice for Carol, but be very careful mate. We don't want to see you coming unstuck.'

Paul suggested that he and Jimmy could do all the ground work on that scumbag for me, such as finding out where he lived, who he hung out with and where he socialised. He said by the two of them doing a bit of research it would make it a lot easier when the time came for me to do what I had to do. This all made good sense to me so I agreed to bring them in on it with me. My brother Vincent wanted me to reassure him that once this all got sorted, it had got to finish. He went on to tell me that I had everything going for me, particularly on the legal side of the business with them. My brother's final words to me were, 'don't fuck it all up for yourself kid!'

This was all good-hearted advice coming from them, and I did appreciate it.

The very next day, as luck would have it, a bombshell really hit home, two gangs of men, calling themselves vigilantes, had been formed in different parts of Manchester. It was blasted all over the northwest news. One of these vigilante gangs even put a name to themselves and wanted to be known as 'The Sheriffs'. A member of one of these gangs was wearing a mask and could be seen on the TV screen talking to a news journalist. The gang member was saying how decent people had had enough of the terror and muggings on their estates, and as he put it, they were formed to sheriff their own community from the thugs and scumbags. After hearing and listening to this my phone started ringing, it was Steve and he was asking if I had I been watching the television, had I heard the news and what did I think? He said to me in an excited voice that he would be down to my place within fifteen minutes.

He arrived together with Chris and Carl. We were all very excited about these events and it was coming up to nine o-clock, which is when the next Northern news bulletin was back on the screen. We all sat there waiting for the outcome in anticipation. When the news finally came on the TV we all got another big surprise, the vigilante stories had now escalated to as far as Birmingham. Myself and the rest of us just couldn't believe what was happening. These events had suddenly; like a chain reaction, gone spiralling right out of control. In some parts of the television news it was actually showing people out on the streets voicing their opinions. Others were stating they had had enough of the yobs and low-life and were swearing that from now on they would be taking the law into their own hands if they had to. I thought to myself, is this a good thing or a bad thing? I don't know.

After seeing and listening the news that day I thought that this could be the start of something. It could turn things around on these lawless ghettos. If this sort of disruption continued God knows what was going to happen. I think it's about time these so called Council Officials and M.P.'s woke up. These are the people, the ones who had been chosen, by the public to represent the people who lived on these run down council estates, weren't they? Something had to be done quickly and effectively; otherwise it looked as if a big time bomb was waiting to go off.

Within the forth-coming weeks it became a regular occurrence to hear about communities in different towns from north to south who were being manned by vigilante gangs. In most cases order and respect was being restored by force and decent people, particularly the pensioners, welcomed it all with open arms. Streets were starting to become safer, muggers and other low-life scum were being severely dealt with in some way or another. We had read in one of the news articles about vigilantes who were operating in some out of the way northern town, they had captured and punished two muggers. This was done by way of a medieval method; Tar and Feathered. The two scumbags were then left chained to a pay machine in the town centre car park. To me, that seems like a well-deserved piece of justice. In some other regions, we had also heard and read, that police forces, political representatives and do-gooders were strongly condemning this vigilante justice, warning the public that law and order would break down.

Well, to me, that was one big joke coming from them. Law and order had already broken down in most of these communities. In my opinion, the police and the rest of those government officials had only themselves to blame. Why had they not seen this coming? All of the warning signs had been there, hadn't they? It wasn't so long back that Liverpool women had been marching in the city streets, some carrying placards. These ladies who had lost loved ones (sons and daughters) through knife and gun crime were calling for action to be taken, but no, it always seemed to all fall on deaf ears. Only recently, protesters joined with various other groups of the public wanting justice. Their cry was, sentences that had been imposed by judges were far too lenient to fit the crime, especially when it concerned women and kids or an old aged person who had been violently abused or in some cases, murdered. The mothers and families of these victims were only asking for one thing.....Justice..... Justice that they are being denied. I mean let's face it, when one of those vicious crimes were or had been committed, sometimes it could take up to an hour for the police to arrive. By the time they did arrive, the violent attack could have already been carried out and the attacker had long gone.

I mean lets be fair; what priorities come first with the police? We have all read and heard about pathetic blunders that do go on amongst some police forces. When these so called mistakes do happen, questions have to be answered. The police come up with very lame excuses: *we don't have the man power* or *we were attending to a more serious matter*. A more serious matter? That's a joke. How many times have we all seen a trivial road accident happen?

Let's say, for example, two cars have bumped into each other, the damage might be a broken headlight or plastic bumper etc. What happens next? A miracle! From out of nowhere and within minutes police cars suddenly appear. Sometimes there could be as many as two or three, who have raced to the scene, and let's not forget; some of these police cars are not road traffic vehicles. Anyway, picture the scene: they have arrived at the road accident that they will describe as a very serious matter. In no time at all they start to take statements from witnesses, measuring the road, sometimes slowing down the oncoming traffic, which inevitably causes congestion. Now during this precious police time, what is taking place elsewhere? There could be a person who has phoned the police for help, and is about to be attacked. The area where the said attack is taking place might only be a few minutes away from the scene of the car accident. But help is not coming, simply because the police are attending a more serious matter. Now I am not suggesting that this is a regular occurrence with the police, I am only describing a trivial road accident here, not a major one, but this preference and choosing who they attend to first *does* go on. I think the public are quite aware of these happenings and are also aware that some of the police are renowned for getting their priorities wrong.

I have heard that there is more to it; for instance some bizzies don't want to know when they receive a violent call out, the simple reason being that some of them are too scared to front up. So have they got their priorities right? And if so, what the fuck is happening? I can go on and on criticizing, not only the police, but also council officials and the rest of those political representatives, we all can, but do they take any real action when there is a cry for help? I don't think so.

It seems to me that a large percentage of those officials are not interested, nor indeed, dedicated to their chosen careers. I really believe they are in the job for one reason only and we all know what that is? Just look at the luxury life styles they all have? Doesn't that say it all? It is a known fact that they have even brought out various rules to suit themselves. One of the blue print schemes they brought out is equality, equality that's a laugh it should have been called diversity. I am starting to wind myself up over these people who are supposed to be representing the public. To me, a majority of these are liars and cheats, is it any wonder that everything seems to be in a mess? Anyway, enough of my political views and opinions, I will get back to my story......

Almost a year had gone by since my friends and I formed our own vigilante team. When the four of us first got our heads together we all knew what we would be letting ourselves in for if anything went wrong along the way. It was a difficult decision to make at the time, but after weighing up all the pro's and con's, we went for it. I was determined to rid the community I once knew and grew up in, of the low-life scum. So with our dedication, perseverance and patience, it all sort of paid off. The Wood Green estate was now a much safer place for decent people to live. I knew we hadn't cleaned up the streets entirely and there were still a few scumbags hanging around, but they knew that if any of them ever did get out of hand, we would be back!

These days I was now living a normal healthy life. My two loyal friends, Paul and Jimmy together with my brothers had sort of taken me under their wing. I was now working straight for a living, well if you can call it that. It's funny, thinking back some years ago, the five of us would be planning and doing all kinds of graft, such as blags, safe jobs etc. Now here we all were years later working honestly and paying our taxes. This new way of life I now had felt so good, and I wanted to keep it that way. I still kept in regular contact with young Steve, Carl and Chris. Just before we disbanded our little team, we made a pact, vowing that if ever the low-life started any of their antics around the community again we would quickly regroup and go and sort them out. Anyway we left it at that, Steve and the others had chilled out, and they were all doing fine these days. They all had little businesses now and were living clean healthy lives. I still went to visit Carol and Frank quite regularly and sometimes I called on the couple that ran the newsagents, Mr and Mrs Khan, they were two very nice hard working people. I was also doing a lot more socialising now. Tracey, the girl I met a couple of months ago, was back on the scene. We both sort of hit it off when we met up again. So yeah, I was living a good, clean honest life together with my loyal friends and family, who I love. I couldn't ask for anything more... but then when you least expect it, things can change!

CAROL'S JUSTICE

'I came face to face with him John; he was pointed out to me and Paul. We have also found out where he lives?'

It was Jimmy telling me that he and Paul had located the whereabouts of the animal that had brutalised Carol. His name was Nathan Clark. At last I had got this scumbag placed, but it was not going to be easy copping for him. Jimmy went on to tell me that this low-life had moved up in the world, he was also rapidly making a name for himself. He was now a street pusher (distributor of drugs) and he was doing it in a fairly big way. He also lived in an expensive pad with his girlfriend.

This is all part and parcel of the way these low-life scumbags make their way to the top of the ladder, from a violent low-life street animal. When an opportunity comes along to work for the big dealers they grab at it.

I was also told that this animal was tooled up at all times and always had a few bodies hanging around with him. This was where I had to be extra vigilant; I needed to attack this bastard when he was alone.

When Jimmy and Paul gave me this information they were begging me not to do it on my own they wanted to come right in on it with me. I told them both that I really appreciated their offer but, this was my little war and I could handle it. Jimmy wasn't having any of it and kept insisting that he and Paul needed to watch my back. He said,

'Don't you realise John you're not dealing with young vandals and muggers here, this animal is in with the big fella's now, and if they had any sort of inclination that you were going to cop for him they would get somebody to put a fuckin' bullet in your head.'

Jimmy was dead right in what he was saying, the dealers wouldn't be thinking this was a personal vendetta I wanted for Carol. No, they would think I was another back stabber who was trying to rip them off for their gear (drugs). I was already aware of this. Call me stubborn or plain fuckin' stupid, but my mind was made up; it had to be my way, meaning I would be going solo on this one. There was one last favour I asked of Paul and Jimmy? I needed to see this animal in person so they both agreed that they would point him out to me.

I remember when I first set eyes on that scumbag it was in some pub he regularly visited, I was literally standing a couple of feet away from him. The place was fairly packed at the time I think he was in the company of a woman and some other couple, but I wasn't taking much notice of them, it was just him I was concentrating on, he was about five foot nine inches in height and I would say his age at a guess was early thirties. He had short cropped mousy hair, and, by looking at his build, he was definitely juiced up (on steroids) the vest he was wearing gave him away; it was designed to show off his arms which were heavily tattooed. He looked exactly what he was, with his fat ugly face…. an advanced low-life thug. I got a good I.D. of him that night which stayed implanted in my brain.

My next move was to sit off where he lived. Jimmy and Paul had already pointed his place out to me. He lived in some big old detached house that had been converted into flats. The house being alongside others, some of which were terraces was situated in a big old Victorian park. This public park was circular in design and had a very large lake in the centre of it. It also had a wide footpath edged with bushes and trees. The footpath went all the way around the side of the lake. There was also a very wide two-way road system that went all the way around the inside of this once magnificent park. All of this to me was just perfect. I could sit off in a small van by his place, which incidentally, and like the rest of the houses in the park, was all designed facing the lake. I knew I wouldn't arouse suspicion being in the area because there were plenty of other cars parked stretching all around the circular road.

A couple of days later I had sat off in the van outside of his place, waiting patiently and watching to see this animal's every move. For the first couple of days of my surveillance I had seen his comings and goings and I had noticed that he drove a black Lexus sports car and sometimes a couple of his associates would call around. On one of these occasions all three of them had come out of his apartment and walked from the front of his entrance and across the wide road to where I was parked. They passed by me, what could only have been a couple of metres away. I watched them and they started to walk along the park footpath, eventually drifting away out of my sight. How brazen is that? Here we have a no-mark scumbag, who only a short while ago was beating and stealing from poor decent people, and now he had turned big time, all because he got an invite into selling the other gear. He now thinks he is untouchable, driving around in his Lexus sports car and living in an up market pad. No wonder his sort didn't reign very long, they always bring it on top for themselves, particularly when they are not used to having large amounts of money. They just couldn't control their boasting. It was only a matter of time before the other people (bizzies) put their tabs on him, then it would be the nicking job. Not though, until I get to him first. I hated him with a vengeance, and when I did get this animal, I fully intended to make that much of a mess of him; he would be wishing he was dead.

It had been nearly four days now since I had been on this scumbag's case and so far not once had I ever seen him on his own. I started to wonder to myself... how the fuck was I going to get this low-life bastard? I am a man who has plenty of patience, but this was starting to do my head in. I had been sitting on and off for a few hours on this particular night and it was coming up to seven o'clock. I thought to myself, I better leave it for tonight and see what tomorrow brings. I started the engine of the van up ready to do one, but just as I was about to drive away, I saw him come out of his entrance alone. He was wearing a tracksuit, trainers and a cap. He skipped across the road and onto the park, and then he started jogging away along the footpath. I waited a couple of minutes then slowly drove after him. When I caught up with him he was still jogging away. I drove the van past him and quickly drove around the circular road and parked back where I originally was. Sitting in my van a few minutes later I was watching through my rear view mirror, I caught sight of him jogging around the bend and coming towards me, he then carried on past were I was parked and started to do another lap around the park. I thought to myself, 'another lap, what's this prick on?' This time I didn't follow him I just sat in the van and waited till he had finished, he must have done four laps. I just hoped he was a creature of habit and that this was one of his routines. It did turn out that he did his jogging on a regular basis and more importantly he was almost bang on time every evening.

The night I decided to have him I knew I would need an extra hand. I didn't need any help to do the damage to him (that was the easy part) I had to have a wheelman; somebody to drive me away from the area pretty fast. It was obvious and unavoidable that I would be covered in some forensics after I had finished with this animal. I explained the situation to Jimmy and Paul, they both wanted to drive for me but I insisted I only needed one of them. I took Paul along; he was ideal for this sort of work as he had plenty of patience like myself, which I admired about him. Jimmy, on the other hand, could be a little erratic at times, I'm not knocking him for that, he is loyal and as game as they come, but this had to be done my way.

A couple of nights later Paul and I were sitting off not too far away from the scumbags flat watching and waiting. We had changed the small van I had been using, just in case. It was now getting very close to the time when this animal did his jogging session, but then, it started to rain and I thought 'that's all we need, the rain could fuck this whole operation up.' There was no sign of him coming out of his apartment and the time was starting to drag by. As we both waited, he still didn't show. I had been all geared up for this night. Paul who was sitting behind the wheel and as cool as ever said,

'Take it easy John, he might come out, he's only been ten minutes over due and at least we know he's still in there.'

We could see the Lexus was still parked up outside the place,

'Yeah I know he's still in there, but what about this fuckin' rain?'

'Don't worry about the rain,' Paul said, 'it's only a drizzle.'

That's Paul for you, always optimistic.

Another ten minutes went by and just as I was contemplating that the scumbag wasn't going to show…. out he came. He was fully dressed in his jogging gear, he trotted across the wide road onto the footpath of the park and away he went doing his pacing out. I breathed a sigh of relief when this happened; we already knew he did about three or four laps. My plan was to wait until he was on his third lap; by that time his pace would have slowed right down and most of his energy would have been sapped. Paul and I were still sitting off watching him jogging around the park footpath; by this time he was getting ready to start his third lap. My adrenaline started to pump fast and the hatred in my thoughts suddenly took over me at what I was about to do to this animal. I felt like a mixed cocktail waiting to explode.

I sprang into action not long after he passed the van doing his third lap. I told Paul I would get this bastard just before he completes what would be, his last lap. I got out of the van dressed in a full sporty looking tracksuit and cap, I had black leather skin tight gloves on and was carrying a deadly weapon, it is what's known as a whip cosh it fits nice and snug in your hand, but with a flick it expands into a steel baton, most of the police forces use these types of weapons quite a lot these days. I also had another vicious tool but that was strapped and concealed under my tracksuit top.

Before I got out of the van I put a phoney pair of glasses on, by phoney, I mean they were just thick black frames with no glass in them. I didn't really need to disguise myself so much, because the way I will whack this scumbag he will never be able to identify me. I gave the nod to Paul; we both knew how to play our parts in this move. I got out of the van and started jogging towards the oncoming target. It's funny the way your mind can think? Just a short while ago I was cursing because of the rain, now here I am thinking to myself, this rain is a blessing in disguise as whilst jogging along I couldn't see anybody else about accept for the odd cyclist cycling past. My golden rule has always been; when about to commit a crime, if anything doesn't look right, don't do it. For example, making sure no witnesses are hanging about, to me that would be an important problem. I would then leave it out and wait until I get another opportunity, but I now thought everything looked ok.

I'm still jogging towards the target, and it was so far so good. Then from around the bend I caught sight of him, he was still quite a good distance away. I was all pumped up with adrenaline now and jogging towards him, the both of us were going to be head on when we reach each other. As he was getting nearer to me, I noticed that he was running on the outside of the footpath, this would be perfect for me with me being on the inside, I could get a better swing at him. There was now about thirty metres between us, I had a quick glance around and could see there was not one soul about. We were getting nearer and nearer to each other. I could now hear his heavy breathing. He was getting burnt out. I had now got tight hold of the steel whip-cosh. I flicked it open just a few metres away from him, he was now ready to pass me...

With my heart racing and the adrenaline pumping faster through my veins I let him have it with full force and it caught him right across the lower part of his face. It lifted him right of his feet and he went down like there was no tomorrow. I looked down at him, his legs were kicking around and I knew he was more or less out, but I gave him another whack to make sure.

I quickly looked around making sure nobody was about, my luck was still holding out. I began to drag him from the footpath and onto where the grass and bushes where. This was ideal for me because I was completely out of sight with him. 'Now *I'm* the predator and this animal is at *my* mercy now.' All the things that he did to Carol filled my head with a feeling that is hard to describe, it was much more than hate. Fortunately for him, with the second whack I gave him, he was completely out of the game (unconscious). I quickly rolled him over and had him lying face down I then pulled his tracky top up revealing his back. I quickly unstrapped my other weapon, it was a razor sharp meat cleaver. I made a promise to myself that this scumbag animal would never walk again, or even function for that matter.

When I was in prison I read quite a lot. One of the subjects I studied, because I am a keep fit fanatic, was the human anatomy. I wanted to paralysed this lowlife so I was going for the lower part of this bastard's spine. He would be paralysed from the waist down. So I proceeded with my brutal violence on this animal. I chopped away at the bottom of his spine, it took less than a minute, and the meat cleaver was so sharp it sliced right through his backbone severing his spinal cord. In that brief moment his whole body shuddered and then he went perfectly still. I straighten myself up and I moved away from the mess I had just created. I could feel the rain getting heavier, I took a quick look around, there was still no sign of anybody. I gathered up my tools and quickly got back onto the footpath, which was a few metres away. I jogged back over to the van where Paul was waiting for me. I had another quick look around before I got inside the motor, I then said to Paul,

'Ok? Let's go!'

When we had driven well away from the area, which had taken only a few minutes, an anonymous phone call was made to the local hospital and the bizzies.

Half an hour later I was as clean as a whistle, anything incriminating on me such as forensics had disappeared. Not one word had been spoken when I carried out that attack and I also knew it was virtually impossible for me to have been identified.

Later on that same night and the following day it was all over the news about a man who had sustained horrific injuries, being found in a park by the police and paramedics.

A Newspaper Headline read:

'BEYOND BELIEF

A young man who is having an evening run in the park is viciously attacked for no apparent reason. According to medical reports, the lower part of his spinal cord has been deliberately severed, possibly by a machete or other sharp bladed instrument. It is understood the young man will never walk again. This sick and senseless act that a fellow human being has done to another, is beyond belief.'

A female crime reporter had written that article. What she had written, was to a certain extent, partly true. It *was* brutal what I had done to that low-life animal, but regarding her saying 'it was done for no apparent reason,' well then that is a different story. It is quite obvious that she is completely unaware of the true reason behind it all. I wonder how that crime reporter would react if she ever did get to know why that *sick and senseless attack,* as she put it was carried out... but do you know what? On second thoughts; I don't give a fuck! I will do whatever it takes to get my revenge. Hate and vengeance when combined, can become a very powerful obsession with me!

Did I have any regrets of what I had done to those lowlife scumbags? No, not at all, in fact I would do it again if I had to. The mission that my friends and I had set out to do was, if I can put it this way...'successful!' We came out of it completely unscathed, none of us sustained any injury, we never had any comebacks, and most importantly, there was not one arrest made against any of us. I think the key to our success was that nobody could ever penetrate our circle.

We always kept it close knit and, because we never socialised with each other, nobody got to know whom we really were. Another important point was that we always targeted the top dog out of each gang. When we did happen to deal with any of the main scumbags it was done quickly and efficiently. On several of those occasions it did cross my mind that if I was ever arrested and charged with any of those violent acts, I would never see daylight again, especially if I was found guilty in a court of law. I shudder at the very thought of it, which takes me back to one night a few weeks previous...

I had been out for the evening with my friends and we had had a few drinks, now I was not one for going on the ale really, but this particular night I got slightly blitzed and arrived home fairly late. I remember waking up in my bed, it was about three in the morning, after having a really bad nightmare; my body was shivering and teaming with sweat. The dream seemed so real, it had been about me being locked away forever inside of a prison cell. Somehow that dream, which still often haunts me, has stayed etched on my mind in a weird sort of a way.

Thank God it was only a dream. I was not going anywhere, I told myself, and there is definitely no way I am ever going to go back to prison. Thankfully all that vigilante business was now behind me. I made a sworn promise to my two brothers and friends that I would end it all and I have. I was almost fifty years old now and too much time had already been wasted in the past. Luckily I had now found this new freedom of life, and hopefully that was the way it was going to stay. It was just too precious too loose!

Priorities

I couldn't believe how time could pass so quickly, it had been almost fourteen months since I first came to live in the city centre. Since that time I had come to notice how rapidly things had changed around there. Property developers and planning officials had transformed the whole look of the city with their new building structures. The progress that had been made in such a short space of time was just incredible. What amazed me were the new apartment blocks that seemed to have sprouted up from nowhere. These luxury living quarters didn't come cheap, the prices varied, starting at thousands to literally millions of pounds.

This got me thinking; why is it that so much money, and I am talking about billions of pounds here, is being ploughed into our big major cities? Council officials alone have spent a fortune on high tech security systems. Cameras are installed practically everywhere and are constantly monitoring everything that moves, there is also a strong police presence. Some of these police are in cars and others are on foot patrol and at a given notice they are ready to steam into action. Since the council brought this powerful deterrent into force, the crime rate in the city centre has fallen rapidly. It was only a couple of weeks back when the police issued a statement to the media, announcing that the city of Liverpool is now one of the safest places to live. I have to admit; I can't knock the council for turning things around for the better, but then thinking about it, everywhere would be a safe place to live if the area was constantly swarming with bizzies, wouldn't it?

It is a very different story all together for the people who live on the fringes of the city and the rest of the surrounding suburbs. There is no safe haven what so ever living in some of those areas. The crime rate on the surrounding suburbs has spiralled right out of control. Mention safe and security on any of those places to people who live there and you would be laughed at. Here is something that I can't get my head around;

There are thousands of people who live on those run down council estates and ghettos, paying their rent and very high rates. When added up it runs into millions, so where does all that money go? It certainly does not get ploughed back into those run down communities. I firmly believe all the cities and big towns in this country, which have been lavishly regenerated by the government and council, are for one purpose only.... The living accommodation of the future! It's strange how things came about from past events, for example, like that old saying? 'What goes around comes around.'

Many years ago the wealthy and influential people moved out of the cities to live in expensive homes, which had been built in the surrounding suburbs. The ones that were not so lucky as to crawl out of the quagmire had no other choice but to stay. A large majority of those people lived in squalid conditions. Due to this way of living they became stigmatised with a degrading name; city slums. As time went by and with some progress, conditions started to improve for the lower working class people, or slums as they were called. Eventually many years later, it was decided by the authorities that they were to be turfed out of the cities in their thousands. They were moved into council owned estates. These massive working class dwellings had been built and scattered around the outskirts of the cities. Funnily enough, some of these council estates had been built more or less next door to the homes of the wealthy people who had moved there years before. Can you imagine the unrest that must have been going on at the time? Here we have the lower class city slums living next door to the upper class. This dramatic effect that the government had brought about had started around the early 1950's to the late 1960's, these new council homes had indoor toilets with bathrooms and were very much appreciated by decent working class people. Other new council facilities were built around these estates such as public swimming baths, play centres and many more social activities that the communities could enjoy. Young children and teenagers of the day came from families with good values and respect, obviously there were certain types of low-life hanging around, but they were frowned upon and mostly ostracised by the local communities.

At the end of the 1970's the great decline had started to kick in, in and around the council estates. The older population blamed this on the drug culture, things started to turn around for the worse, increasing the unruly behaviour of the youth. Were drugs the soul cause of the lawlessness that was about to explode? Every generation seems to blame the next one.

For me, I personally think that the kids growing up in the 1980's had it the hardest: Unemployment was, and still is, rife. Kids were leaving school some with excellent degrees and going straight on to benefits. That alone was soul destroying for some, but worse still, the council had started ripping the hearts out of people's communities. With greedy ambitions and lame excuses the councils started to sell off school playing fields, public swimming baths were getting shut down, youth centres and other important premises that entertained the young were rapidly being demolished. Even some woodlands where kids would play and do a bit of fishing were being ripped up and filled in. All of this can only be describe as legalised vandalism. Of course we all know why this was done, so the greedy councils could sell these vital lands and buildings to private developers.

Thinking back, I remember a well-known Lord by the name of Lord Sefton; his mansion is in West Derby (an area of Liverpool). In the 1970's he bequeathed acres of parks and woodlands for the public to enjoy. My friends and I, being a lot younger at the time used to mess about and do a bit of courting there. After a couple of years passed by, trees were being ripped up and fishponds were getting filled in. In their place, private houses, not council house, were being built all over and encroaching on the once beautiful area. This all being down to the inconsiderate greedy council. I would like to know, and so too would most of the public, who gives them (the council) the God given right to sell off land what was actually donated to the public? Is it any wonder why people are so disillusioned? Like I have mentioned before I don't think it is just drugs that is the cause of today's anti-social behaviour, although I would admit, it does play a vital role. I personally believe that these inconsiderate council officials are a lot to blame for the cause of it all. Let's have it right, what is there left for teenagers who live on these run down estates, absolutely nothing. They have been denied the amenities that the young generations before them had. It is sort of like taking away the favourite toys from children and telling them you can't play with them anymore. When kids have been deprived through no fault of their own, resentment and rebellion sets in, and as the saying goes, 'one bad apple can turn the rest bad'. It wasn't so long ago lowlifes were only few in number on the estates, now there are thousands. This violent lawless way of life is not going to get any better, in fact it will go from bad to worse. These days the government and the rest of those high-ranking officials don't seem to be bothered one bit over it all. It seems to me that they are only concerned for the welfare and security of the cities. I am being honest when I say it is safe and secure living here. People can go to sleep at night without having to worry if some lowlife is going to smash your windows or set fire to your home. It is not so for a large number of decent people who live on run down estates and ghettos. What chance have they got? I think the only option for them, if they can afford it, is to buy or rent a place here in the city, otherwise I'm afraid there is nothing down for them.

THE SAFEST MOVES

The little comfort and peace that my friends and I had brought to our old estate wouldn't last for too long. It would be only a matter of time before those scum bags would start kicking off again, particularly if word got around that we had ceased our activities. I didn't really want to get involved in that violent business again as it was so hard for me to control my temper, and who knows, I could have ended up killing one of those lowlifes. So, rather than me going down that road and coming unstuck, I had decided to try and persuade Carol and old Frank to move away from that area. I didn't think it would be too hard to persuade them, considering what they had both been through. I set about getting it all arranged during the next few weeks, and I explained what I was aiming to do, to my two brothers and also to Jimmy and Paul. They all rallied to help me out with everything. Jimmy put me on to a person who always has a lot of pull with some housing trust company that had a residential development in its own private grounds for the elderly.

I went to have a look at the place with the guy who's name was Billy. Billy showed me around the new site, which consisted of little semi-detached one-bedroom bungalows. I thought this was ideal for Frank, but what really put the icing on the cake for me was that the place was highly secured with a twenty-four hour warden watch on site. This would be ideal for old Frank he could live there out of harm's way. Billy set about getting things sorted, and after pulling a few strings here and there regarding the paper work etc, he eventually got it all boxed off for us. Billy turned out to be a decent human being; he wouldn't even take a back-hander from me, which was a nice few quid. Old Frank, the war pilot and one of my heroes as a kid, will live out his time in peace and quiet at last.

My next move was to get Carol sorted out. I thought the best and safest place for her to live would be in the city centre. I could easily get her a nice one-bedroom apartment to rent, preferably by me, which would only be a matter of minutes from my place. To think that almost twelve months had passed by since I first drove into our old estate and knocked on the front door of Carol's house. I remember how frail and ill she looked on that first day, but now, twelve months on, not only has her appearance greatly improved, but so too have her health and mind. She seemed so full of life these days and every time we met she appeared happy and was always laughing. I would say she had almost fully recuperated after that terrible ordeal she went through. The disfigurement that the scumbag did to her eye socket didn't look too bad really. A skilful surgeon from a good private hospital could soon put that right. I know I have started to have a feeling of closeness towards Carol. I knew it was not through pity that I had this feeling for her, but somehow my emotions had started to become strong in a warm sort of a way.

Before I started having these feelings towards Carol I had been seeing quite a lot of Tracey, a younger girl I had meet a few months back. We had been having a good time together and everything, but then I began to realise that the age difference was stretched way too far. There is almost a twenty year gap between us, she being twenty-nine and me forty-nine. Although Tracey was in no doubt a beautiful looking woman, the problem was our relationship; it just didn't have what it takes. At times it was so difficult just trying to converse with her, it also lacked good co-ordination. I think the only good thing about our relationship was the physical side we had for each other. Now that was just something else, even though she had me worn out at times. After a while I knew deep down, and so did she, there was no future in us being together. Tracey was in the theatre business and being young and talented she did have a good career ahead of her. Hanging out with me could jeopardise all that for her, so I had to let her go.

When I was in Carol's company however, everything felt so right I suppose that's because we were both on the same wavelength. Carol and I grew up and hanged around together with the rest of the kids that lived on our estate at the time, so we did have a lot in common due to that. I'm starting to reminisce here but I remember the first date I had with Carol.

I must have only been about fifteen years old, we both had been to see a movie called Grease, all the kids at that time were raving about it, and after seeing the movie I began walking Carol home. I remember it was summer time at around half past ten in the evening and it had just gone dark. We both had stopped by some private houses not too far from our estate; we used to call these the posh houses when we were kids. They were all built on a wide avenue, which had grass verges and were lined with big trees. Anyway, I was leaning against one of the trees with Carol having a bit of a smooch then we stopped for a moment and she asked me what time it was. I didn't have a watch so I couldn't say, she then said to me if it has gone past twelve o'clock it would be her fifteenth birthday. I didn't know if I should wish her a happy birthday or what. I remember having my arms around her waist and I was looking over her shoulder into one of the posh house's front garden, I took my arms away from her and told Carol not to open her eyes for a moment. She giggled and said ok. I quickly paced across the grass verge and I vaulted over the garden fence of the posh house. The garden was full of different types of flowers and the borders were a sea of colour with a whole variety of flowers. I quickly set about picking some of them and after selecting a good bunch I vaulted back over the fence.

Carol, still with her back to me said, 'John what are you doing?'

I told her to open her eyes and turn around. When she saw the flowers her eyes and mouth opened wide, I passed them to her and said, 'Happy Birthday!'
She laughed. 'John, you're mad!'

I nodded to her and said, 'I know I am.'

We were both standing a bit awkward; she holding the flowers and me with my hands in my pockets, when suddenly we heard a loud voice shout. It was coming from an upstairs window in one of the posh houses, the very house from which I had just taken the flowers. Carol and I looked up at the window. I couldn't tell whether it was a man or a woman there, but they were shouting down at us both, something about stealing the flowers.

We didn't hang around to hear anymore, we just legged it like mad down the avenue. Carol was still clutching the flowers.

When we were out of sight we stopped to get our breath back, Carol got the giggles, which set me off. We just couldn't stop laughing, nearly pissing ourselves. A few moments later and our laughter suddenly stopped. We were just about to enter our estate when a police car, which seemed to have come from nowhere, pulled up at the side of Carol and me. Two uniformed bizzies got out of the car and one of them told us to stop, which we did. One of the bizzies looked down his nose at Carol who was still holding the bunch of flowers. The policeman said to her,

'Ok where did you get those flowers from?'

Before Carol could answer I quickly interrupted and told the bizzies that I had bought them for her, I added it is her birthday. I started to explain to them both that we had been to the movies...

'You are a little liar,' the other bizzie said. 'We know you stole them from a person's garden and I am arresting you for theft.'

To cut a long story short, I held my hands up, telling them Carol had nothing to do with it all. They just bungled me into the police car together with the flowers. One week later I was up in front of a magistrate's court on a charge of pilfering flowers. I was fined the grand sum of two pounds! Both my parents had to come to court with me because I was under age. That was in 1970, could you imagine that happening today?

It was now 2005, and tomorrow was Carol's birthday. I had ordered from the local florist in the city, a beautiful bouquet of flowers for her. This time I would get it right and I would pay for them honestly instead of robbing them, the way I had all those years ago when I was just a kid. For a moment I was still deep in thought and reminiscing about the way things used to be, when suddenly I was brought back to the present by my mobile phone ringing. I answered it and it was Steve.

'John,' he shouted down the phone to me. 'There has just been a news bulletin about three vigilantes getting shot by a gang of scumbags. One of them got it right in the head and was killed outright. The poor bastard had a wife and two kids. It happened somewhere around Manchester.'

I told Steve that I would put the T.V on and see if I could get an update on it. Later on I got the full story about it all:

It appeared it had happened on a council estate, which was situated on the outskirts of Manchester. According to some eyewitnesses, a big furniture removal van had driven onto the said estate and had pulled up by a gang of yobs. It was believed that this particular gang were notorious, especially for their violent muggings and other serious street crimes. Anyway, a large number of men had quickly jumped out of the rear of the van and had steamed into the gang of scum. They then proceeded to knock fuck out of them. Like the rats these scum are, some of them ran away and it seemed as if the vigilantes had come out on top, but soon afterwards the scum where back with a larger group of reinforcements. Some of them had brought killer dogs back with them on chains. A friend of mine, who was from that part of Manchester, filled me in on what had really taken place there.

He told me it was the most vicious street fight he had ever seen. The scum were armed with machetes, knives etc. Blood was flowing everywhere and the vigilantes where starting to come badly unstuck. What finalised it all was that one of the scumbags, who was armed with a gun, started firing indiscriminately into the vigilantes, shooting three of them. Two were seriously wounded and the other one was shot dead. When it was all over the bizzies arrived on the scene; as always they got there too late. When you think about it, unless the police actually catch these people in the act, they have no chance what so ever of getting a conviction. Especially when the perpetrators have disposed of any real evidence.

Later that evening Steve called to my place, he had also brought along Chris and Carl. Apparently, Steve knew a couple of the vigilantes who had taken part in that vicious street fight. He seemed very upset over it all for some reason or other. I told him to take it easy and to calm himself down.

'Look,' I said. 'We are not involved with that sort of business anymore.'

'I know what you mean John,' he said. 'But those vigilantes were decent men trying to look after their own communities. Just look what's happened to them. The scumbags are using guns now, what chance has anybody got against guns?'

'Yeah I know,' I said trying to calm him down. 'It is unfortunate that a friend of a friend of yours got killed, but remember me telling you all, never go into a street battle with a gang of scum? We always sit off and bide our time, that's our way. At least until the opportunity arises for us to take their main man out.'

I went on to explain how those vigilante guys had gone about it all the wrong way. For one they had put themselves right on offer by not being 'ballied' up. They didn't wear masks. That was a big mistake on their part. It put them in a dangerous position, where they could be identified. Thus, they put their houses and families in jeopardy and at risk of revenge from those lowlifes.

Just before our little meeting was over I reminded Steve,

'What happened on that estate in Manchester has got nothing to do with any of us what so ever. If those and other vigilantes want to operate that way by making serious mistakes and coming unstuck then that's their own fault as far as I am concerned. The four of us sitting here have more or less cleaned our own estate up. How long it will it stay like that? Who knows! But I can reassure the three of you that if our estate *does* start to get out of hand, we can always get together again and get it sorted.'

We all agreed and left it at that. It was late in the evening by the time the discussion had ended. Carl and Chris, who had been sitting quietly throughout all of this for some reason or other, didn't have much to say. Maybe it was because of Steve's agitated behaviour, he had just kept repeating himself and wouldn't shut up.

When they finally left my place, it *did* get me thinking, particularly over the shooting of the three vigilantes. I was determined it wouldn't happen to any of our crew if there were any more kick-offs with that scum who were left on our old estate, not if I could help it.

I do think, in fact I am convinced, that street wars, which by now are rapidly escalating in and around council estates all over this country, are here to stay for quite a long time. When will it all end? Who knows. It was only a few months back we started hearing about street gangs shooting and killing each other. Now that didn't bother me at all, scum on to scum bumping one and other off. What I *am* against

and so too are the public, is that now lowlife gangs are turning their guns on decent people.
Some of those drugged-up crazy bastards are shooting indiscriminately, and in some cases, women and kids have been caught up in the crossfire. This is all because clean living people are trying to make their communities safe. Like I have mentioned before, what is the outcome of it all going to be? God knows! It seems that this has become a war, street wars, a war between good and evil.

The following morning, as usual, I was up bright and early. I called in at the local florist for the bouquet of flowers I had ordered, for Carol's birthday.

After doing this I went to have a coffee with Steve and Paul. They had an office in the city centre. I did this quite often, paying them a visit, offering to help out here and there. After all, the two of them, and my brothers had put me on wages. There were times when I felt embarrassed over this, because to me, it seems as though I was doing nothing to earn this good salary. I had on many occasions tried to explain this to Steve, Paul and my two brothers, but they wouldn't have it any other way. So there I was having a nice hot coffee and sat around the table with those two honourable men. We were all sat having a bit of a laugh, Jimmy was wisecracking as he usually did. Eventually the conversation turned to the shootings of the three vigilantes.

'It was bang out of order John,' said Jimmy. 'What one of those slimy rats did; shooting a decent man dead in broad daylight.'

'I know,' said Paul. 'It's going from bad to worse. Those scum bags are too scared to have a straightener so instead they shoot one another in the back and then they run away, the fuckin cowards.'

It is true what Jimmy and Paul was on about; these days there is no such thing as two fellas having it-off one-on-one. Even a gang onto a gang fighting each other out on a field somewhere is to a certain extent acceptable, but that just doesn't happen anymore. The gun is the choice of weapon for settling scores these days. Well if this is the way it has got to be, using guns on the streets, I don't want to know.

After we had finished our coffee and everything I stood up to make a move. Jimmy asked what my plan for the day was. I explained to him about Carol and how I was going to talk her into moving to the city centre by me. I also told them it was her birthday today and I was on my way to the estate to see her. I had started to ramble on about Carol, when Jimmy and Paul started smiling at me. Jimmy said to me, laughing,

'Don't tell us you're going to marry her after all these years?'

'Hey,' I replied, laughing back at them both. 'One marriage was enough for me.'

Jimmy told me he wasn't doing anything that day and that he would come with me to our old estate. 'If that's ok?' He asked.

'Yeah, sure,' I replied smiling.

We both left Paul in the office telling him we would catch him later. Getting in my car, Jimmy noticed the flowers on the backseat. He looked at the flowers then back at me.

'It looks like this could be love John,' he said, laughing again.

'Don't be silly; it's her birthday,' I quickly replied.

Thinking about it though; Jimmy could be right.

On the drive up to the estate I started explaining to Jimmy the way I was beginning to feel towards Carol, and how she had made good progress regarding that terrible ordeal she had been through. Jimmy just sat there listening for a change as I went on talking; telling him how radiant Carol looked and how she was always laughing and seemed dead happy. He turned to me and said,

'John I understand, and if that's what you want, I am made up for you.'

We were about to pull up outside Carol's house.

'Just wait until you see her Jim,' I said, 'she has completely changed for the better.'

We both got out of the car, me holding of the bouquet of flowers. As I rang the front door bell I thought to myself; 'this will surprise her'.

After ringing for a little while with no response, Jimmy looked at me and shrugged. I thought, 'this is a bit strange, where is she?' We both started to walk away down her path, when I heard knocking from an upstairs window of the house. I looked up and saw it was Carol. She looked very upset. I indicated to her to come down and open the door.

I said to Jimmy. 'Something's not right here, I can just feel it.'

Carol opened the door; she looked absolutely petrified. She was trembling and trying to tell me something in a hoarse voice. I passed the flowers to Jimmy and grabbed hold of her. We went inside the house, Jimmy closing the front door behind us all. I started trying to calm her down, but by now she had become hysterical. She kept repeating,

'I saw him, I saw him, and his eyes were staring at me, his horrible piercing eyes. John he is going to kill me I know he is.' She was really sobbing.

'Nobody is going to kill you,' I said quietly. 'I'm here now and nobody will hurt you Carol.'

She was shivering and clinging to me like a baby. I looked over at Jimmy who was just standing there shaking his head.

'It seems there's one thing after another doesn't it?' He said.

I was thinking to myself; what a setback this was, Carol was practically over that violent ordeal she had been through with that lowlife animal. All the good progress she had made over the past twelve months had all been undone. I went on comforting her, and after a short while, she finally calmed down.

She then went on to reveal to Jimmy and I what had taken place that morning.

Apparently, she had gone to the local post office taking Kate her little dog with her for the walk. On arriving at the post office, and before she entered, Carol decided to pick her dog up as it was only tiny (a miniature jack Russell) and take it in with her. She joined a small queue of customers inside and waited her turn. Whilst waiting she noticed there was a man to her far left sitting in a wheelchair. Carol sort of glanced over at the invalid man who was now staring at her with an evil look on his face. She froze as she realised who he was. Clutching her little dog, which she had tucked under her arm, she tried to look away but it was to no avail. His wheelchair was positioned directly in front of her on the opposite side of the room. Carol went on to tell us that he then started psyching her out, he pointed at her little dog, indicating with his hand, he mouthed that he would cut its throat. By now Carol's nerves had completely gone, she turned still clutching her little dog and ran out of the place. It turned out it was the same scumbag who had violently attacked her and killed her other dog two years before.

When she had finished telling us I was seething with hatred for that animal. I couldn't believe how that rat, after what I had done to him, hadn't learnt his lesson. Having been put in a wheelchair and out of action the scumbag was still at his terror antics. It's quite obvious Carol didn't know it was me who was solely responsible for making a mess of him. I knew now I had to act quickly and get her away from this estate. Who knows? That lowlife could get some other scumbag to attack her and that would be the end for her, as it would finish her this time. I was just about to explain to Carol my idea of her moving away from the estate when she took the words right out of my mouth.

'John, I don't want to live around here anymore, I'm scared. I just know he is going to kill me, I could tell by his eyes.'

Again she broke down sobbing.

Jimmy looked at me and said, 'Let's get her out of this hole, John.'

I nodded in agreement. I told Carol she wouldn't be spending another night here, and to start packing any gear needed for the night as she could stay at my place. She then asked,

'What about Kate?'

I told her she was coming with us too.

'Don't worry about the rest of your gear love,' Jimmy said to Carol. 'I can get a couple of my men to pick it all up and have it stored at one of my places.'

Once this was all decided, Jimmy wanted me to drive him down to his office, as he had some business to attend too. I told Carol I wouldn't be more than an hour then I would be back to pick her up. After reassuring her and saying our goodbyes, Jimmy and I got into my car and I drove away down the street. When I came to the bottom of the street I did a right turn into the main avenue that runs through the estate. As I was driving down the avenue I noticed a fella in a wheelchair on the opposite side, Jimmy had spotted him too.

'I'm sure that's the fuckin' animal we've just been on about,' I said to Jimmy.

Jimmy asked if I was certain it was him so I drove slowly past. When we got abreast of him I looked across and instantly recognised him.

'Are you sure it's him?' Jimmy asked me.

'Yeah I'm fuckin' sure; I never forget an enemy's face, and certainly not that animal's.'

'You can't do anything here John, it's broad daylight,' Jimmy said. 'You know the score, witnesses around, there could even be bizzies knocking about.'

'Hey Jimmy,' I said getting a bit annoyed. 'Give us some credit, I'm not that fuckin' stupid, to get myself nicked for that scumbag.'

205

As I drove past the animal and got to the top of the street, I decided to do a u-turn. I then proceeded to drive back towards the wheelchair scumbag who was still on the opposite side. I pulled the car up about ten meters away from him and quickly started getting out of my car.

'For fuck's sake John,' shouted Jimmy startled. 'What are you doing?'

I told him to stay put in the motor and that I would only be a couple of minutes.

'Don't worry,' I said. 'Nothing is going to happen.'

I quickly crossed over to the other side of the street and started trotting after the wheelchair. Jimmy was right, there was quite a bit of activity going on at that time, some people where walking passed on the sidewalk, there was also a fair bit of traffic passing by. I had no intention what so ever of doing any damage once I had caught up with him, no way; I wasn't so stupid as to stick my neck out. I was just going to have a quick and quiet little talk to him!

Moments later I slowed down; I was only about four or five meters away from him. I walked briskly up to the back of his wheelchair and pulled it to a stop with both my hands.

The scumbag muttered something like *what the fuck* as he tried to turn his head around.

With my arms positioned on either side of the chair I leaned forward towards the back of him and spoke with a low and menacing voice into his ear.

'Don't try and turn around cunt,' I said to him. 'Just listen to what I have got to say, you fuckin' dog. I was the one who put you in that chair! Yeah me.'

He then mumbled something and tried to move his head again, but he couldn't because I had the side of my head against his by now. I went on talking to him as he sat there shaking.

'The next time I get you; and I can get you anytime I want, I am going to cut the two eyes out of your fuckin' head so you won't be able to see, never mind not being able to walk. Have you listened carefully to what I've just said to you?'

He then mumbled something out of his mouth, which I didn't take in.

I straightened myself up and told him not to turn around. My final words to him were:

'Now fuck off in your pram away from me you bag of shit. Go on, and get the fuck out of my sight. You might want your nappy changing, you fucking stink you scumbag.'

I stood for a few seconds and watched as he started pushing himself away. I then turned around and trotted back down the street to my car. Jimmy still sitting in the passenger seat asked me as I got in.

'Everything alright John?'

'Yeah,' I replied, 'there won't be any more fuckin' about from him ever again, I gave him some strong verbal and the dirty bastard went and shit himself.'

Jimmy burst out laughing after I had told him. I started the motor up and we drove away. I meant every word of what I had said to that lowlife scum, I wouldn't have thought twice about blinding him at all for what he had put Carol through, and do you know what? I would feel no remorse what so ever. To me that type of scumbag shouldn't be alive.

It was a few days later that I had Carol and her little dog living with me safe and sound in my place. When I come to think about me moving Carol into my place, I hadn't realise but it was what I really needed, the good company of a clean decent woman. As daft as it may seem, even Kate, her little dog, was also good company to have around the place too. To me this seemed a perfect sort of home life.

Loneliness can be a very unpleasant experience for some people. I know it was for me, especially when I was locked away in prison for several years. Most nights in my cell I used to pine for the simplest things in life, simple things like those I used to take for granted. These days though I appreciate everything that is handed to me because it's the simple things in life that money can't buy, like for instance Carol and I, together with the dog, go for walks along the waterfront.

Liverpool waterfront is a magnificent sight to behold and experience these days. Just to stroll along this part of the city and take in the fresh air by the side of the river is, I find, a good way to chill out.

When I was a kid, the River Mersey was so polluted, dark and murky; it was such a depressing place to see. This of course, was all down to the big factories and warehouses that seemed to stretch for miles along the docks.

Most of these big old buildings used and abused the river by disposing of their waste into it, which inevitably over the years, completely contaminated the water. These modern days, due to the environmental authorities, things have changed for the better.

A big clean-up project got started by dredging the riverbeds. Now the water is practically free of contamination, even fish, I am told, are starting to thrive in the river. It's funny, when I was first informed about the cleaning up of the Mersey, I used to wonder if anything of interest was ever found by any of the men working on the project at the time. I mean, what I am getting at, is that my friends and I, when we were at the other business many years ago, used to use the river ourselves to get shut of anything we didn't want. There has been many an occasion we have thrown the odd safe into it, always empty of course. Around that era, during the 1970's, it was common knowledge, amongst the criminal fraternity in Liverpool, if you wanted to get shut of anything for example, disposing of any incriminating evidence that could get you nicked, you simply dumped it in the Mersey. Yeah, I bet the bed of that old river must hold some secrets from years gone by.

It had been almost eighteen months since I was released from prison, and in that time, I had felt that there was something still missing in my life. It was something I couldn't seem to put my finger on. I now realised I had finally found what I had been searching for.... it was called contentment! These days Carol and I had started to plan our future together and hoped like the old saying goes, we could both live a happy ever after.

Sometimes though, things don't work out the way you thought they would, and the plans that you have made can turn out drastically wrong. I don't think there is a man on this planet that can be so sure as to know what his future holds for him. Even Nostradamus himself failed to get all his predictions accurate.

For instance, take myself, I would never have thought in less than one week from now I would be charged with three murders. They were murders that were, according to what the police described, cold-blooded killings. This is how the last part of my story goes:

THE BUILD UP

It all began one Saturday evening. Carol and I were sat in a restaurant in the city, with my two brothers and their girlfriends. The restaurant had a good reputation and was renowned for its excellent food and wine. We hadn't ordered our meals yet as we were waiting for our friends, Jimmy and Paul to arrive with their other halves (girlfriends). When I think back about that Saturday evening it seemed odd, because I never gave it a thought up until then but, my two brothers Jimmy and Paul were in the same boat as myself. We were all divorced or separated from our wives, hence the new girlfriends. Anyway, here we all were ready to enjoy ourselves, meeting up on Saturday evening and having a good night on the town. By the way, it did become a regular occurrence with our crowd, meeting up each Saturday evening.

After a while Jimmy and Paul eventually showed up with their girlfriends. They were slightly late so Paul apologised. So too did Jimmy, who said he was sorry but the delay was all down to him. I remember Jimmy looked slightly troubled on that Saturday evening, I could tell, as he wasn't his usual jovial self. After we had all eaten our meals the wine began to flow thick and fast. The conversation became a lot merrier; obviously this was all down to the bubbly. Carol and the rest of the women were going good style on the wine and I had also noticed Jimmy had changed back to his old self, becoming the life and soul of the party. I looked around the big dining table where we were all sat and watched our crowd chatting away and laughing. I thought to myself; this is what life is all about, being in the company of people whom I love and trust. I remember it being a warm and pleasant evening on that Saturday night, one I will never forget, because it was to be my last.

At one point, during the course of that evening, Jimmy stood up from where he was sitting and mentioned he was going outside for a smoke. Before he went he looked straight at me. I got on to him right away. That look he gave me was an indication for me to follow him outside. It's weird but when Jimmy and the rest of us used to hang out as kids and even right up until now, we all know each other's mannerisms and habits and particularly what they meant, especially the eyes. A minute or so later I too got up and excused myself from the table. Nobody took a blind bit of notice when I left, they were all too busy laughing and joking with each other. The women, by now though, were looking slightly the worst for wear.

I met up with Jimmy outside of the premises.

'Ok,' I said to him, 'spill it out to me, what's going on?'

'John,' he said to me, 'I didn't want to mention anything to you inside the restaurant just in case anybody, especially the women, overheard anything.'

'Yeah I understand,' I said, 'but come on what is it?'

He went on to tell me about the kidnapping of a fourteen-year-old boy that had taken place on the Wood Green estate (our old estate). Steve had been filling him in on it all, and that was the reason he had been late arriving at the restaurant. He then went on to tell me, Steve, Chris and Carl were making plans to rescue the kid, who according to them had been badly tortured. Hearing this came as a shock to me, because, we had cleaned up our old estate months ago. I then asked Jimmy whether Steve knew the boy and if the bizzies had been informed? We couldn't talk for too long outside the restaurant so he briefly filled me in about it all.

Steve knew the young kid very well, in fact the boy was Steve's younger brother's best friend, and they hung out together. He went on to tell me the young kid was also the son of the Asian couple who ran the local newsagents and off-licence on the estate. As of yet, the bizzies had not been informed, as the boy's parents were too scared to go to the police. The reason being, that the scum who were holding their son had threatened to shoot him dead if the police were involved. To me, Jimmy seemed more concerned over his nephew Steve than he was about the kidnapped boy. He was worried he would come badly unstuck, even as far as getting himself killed if he went ahead trying to rescue the boy. He did say he tried to talk Steve out of the idea but it was to no avail. What was really worrying Jimmy was that this gang were not your average scallies. He told me they were dead heavy and were real nasty bastards with it. He said they wouldn't think twice about putting a bullet in you. He asked me if I would have a word with Steve, 'at least he will listen to you John,' he said.

I told him to forget about it for tonight; tomorrow was another day. I also told him I would arrange a meeting with Steve and the rest of the crew. I even suggested that he should come along and join us at the meeting. By doing it that way we could all get around the table and discuss the matter properly. After I had outlined this to him, he nodded his head and said, 'yeah that's fine by me John.'

'Come on Jim,' I urged him. 'Let's get back inside; the other lot will be wondering where we have got to.'

We both went back inside the restaurant to join our crowd, who were still sitting at the table. The atmosphere amongst them was absolutely buzzing and of course; the wine was definitely flowing well. I remember thinking to myself, here we go again, this is gonna be another one of those crazy Saturday nights; all of us getting tanked-up, only to wake up the next morning suffering with a ruthless hangover. I often wonder how people can become an alcoholic. It is just beyond me. I myself need at least a week, or possibly more, to recuperate after being on a bender.

However, on the Sunday; and just as predicted, not feeling too good, I did manage to arrange a meeting with young Steve and company. It was to be held at my place on the following Monday at about twelve o'clock. I had arranged for Carol to be out of the apartment. I told her that Jimmy would be calling with some friends to discuss a business proposition with me. That was one of Carol's good qualities; she always respected any private meetings I had with my close friends. She was the type of woman who would always make herself scarce with no problem at all. She left about eleven-ish that morning, saying she would catch up on some shopping. Everything was going through my mind on that Monday while I was waiting for my friends to show. I had a gut feeling that something bad was going to happen to me, particularly concerning the kidnapping of the young boy.

It was a feeling I had experienced many times in the past, when we were bang at the other business (crime). I remember my friends and I would be ready to embark on some real heavy graft, for instance a bank raid, a wage blag from a security depot or some other criminal activity. Sometimes, on those occasions I would get a sort of sixth sense, telling me something was not right. Whenever this *did* happen to me, which by the way was not too often, I would quickly tell the rest of our team that we were not going ahead with it. Somehow, I was usually dead right in my calculations. I mean, let's face it, we were all fit young men at that time and for us to come unstuck whilst pulling one of those heavy moves, it would mean doing a long stretch and rotting away in some piss hole of a prison.

Well, that was all back then, now was the present, and I had started to think about what the future might hold for me, well not just for me, for Carol too. I mean we had everything going for the two of us, and it felt so good that I wouldn't have wanted anything to jeopardise it all. After considering all of this I came to a conclusion, I decided there and then that there was no way I would allow myself to be sucked into anymore street violence. In the past couple of months, street wars or street violence had escalated into near anarchy according to the news bulletins on TV and in the papers. Shootings and killings were an everyday occurrence on most council estates up and down the country. There had now been some talk of the government putting armed forces on foot patrol in some of the worst no-go areas. I don't know if it is a good thing or a bad thing that they plan to do, but then maybe at least if they *do* go ahead with it, it could restore some order.

Not too long ago it was only the street thug who would use a gun, but because society has become almost lawless, some decent people who were once law abiding have themselves now taken up arms. They say that they have no alternative. It is the only way to protect their families and homes. Now because they have resorted to this, the police have branded them *Vigilantes*.

I decided that when Steve and the others arrived I would put my cards on the table and tell them what I told them a few months back. I was now finished with the vigilante business and street violence. On the other hand, I would give them all my expertise and my advice on how to go about rescuing the young kid. That was of course if Steve couldn't be talked out of the matter. After all, Jimmy *did* ask me as a favour to try to put Steve off going ahead with his plans.

THE BEST WAY FORWARD

It was bang on twelve o'clock when Steve, Carl, Chris and Jimmy arrived at my place. I was greeted warmly with a firm handshake by each one of them. For the first couple of minutes after they had arrived, a little jovial banter took place between us. Then after getting ourselves seated we immediately got our heads together and the conversation between us became deadly serious. It was Steve who started the ball rolling and got straight to the point. He started to fill me in about how and when the young boy had been kidnapped and tortured. This was the way Steve outlined the story to me: -

It appeared the young boy was snatched by the scum, simply because he was vulnerable, therefore an easy target so to speak. The scumbags also knew about the shop the boy's parents had and also the trickle of money what was going into the cash till each day and night. Now, because of this information, one of the scumbags called to the shop each night without fail and made a pick-up. This was done because the boy's parents could not raise the lousy ten grand that they had demanded in the first place.

As Steve continued explaining this terrible ordeal to me, I could see he was getting very upset over it. It seemed that not only were these animals brutally torturing the boy by cutting off one of his fingers; they took it a step further. They cruelly let the boy's parents listen to their son on a mobile phone, pleading for them to get the ransom money. To prove they were not fuckin' about, the evil scumbags had a go-between who delivered their sons finger to them in a matchbox. I thought I had heard the worst, from what Steve had told me so far, but what he went on to reveal to me next made my skin crawl!

Since the kidnapping of the young boy had taken place, Steve together with Carl and Chris, had done quite a bit of homework on it all. It was believed that the main one of the gang was always tooled up with a shooter. He had a reputation so fierce and evil that his own scumbag associates were themselves wary of him. He was twenty eight years old and was known as 'Sick Mick' but his real name was Michael Dunne. It was common knowledge among the lowlife fraternity that this animal was a paranoid, crack cocaine addict with psychopathic tendencies. He was also a male rapist with a preference for young boys. I thought I had heard the worst, particularly about the mutilation of the kid's finger but after hearing the boy is at the mercy of that depraved psycho, it just made me more determined to get things sorted one way or the other. Throughout this meeting I had noticed the way Jimmy, Carl and Chris sat quietly listening to what Steve had been telling us, it was quite obvious that it had affected them too.

At this point in the meeting, I suggested we should all have a break with some tea or coffee. I got up from my chair and went into the open-plan kitchen area to arrange the drinks. I thought hard about what Steve had told me and it made me feel sick to my stomach. I had started to pour the drinks out, when Jimmy came over to me.

'What do you think about it John?' he asked with concern.

'It's bad Jim; in fact it's fuckin' disgusting what I've just heard.'

I looked around at Jimmy and the rest of my friends. They all seemed on a downer.

A few minutes later, and after we had finished our drinks, I asked Steve why he was so keen to get involved in all of this. He told me that his younger brother Davey was the best friend of the kid; whose name by the way was Amir, it then dawned on me just who this kid was, as I had spoken recently to his parents in the shop. I realised that this was a good, clean living, well-mannered kid. Steve went on to tell me that the two boys were never separated and they always hung out together. He also said that he and his wife were very good friends of the boy's parents, Mr & Mrs Khan. Apparently, they had approached Steve when the boy was first abducted and not knowing whom they could turn to they had asked Steve for help. The police were out of the question because of the death threats from the scumbags. It was believed, every time the boy made a phone call to his parents, the scumbag 'Sick Mick' had a gun pointing to his head.

'OK Steve,' I said. 'I understand where you're coming from and how you feel about it all. If you, Carl and Chris are to go ahead with your plans, have you realised the consequences of what you are up against? After all, that sick psycho bastard who is running the show is not only armed with a gun, but according to what we have heard, he will use it. Let's face it Steve, what chance has any of you got against a shooter?'

The three of them nodded back in agreement with me. I was only putting it this way to Steve to try to deter them from going ahead with the rescue, as Jimmy had asked me to do. But for all the talking and persuading I was trying to get across, I could see it was having no effect on them, especially Steve.

Jimmy, who was seated and had been listening very intently, suddenly stood up looking agitated and shouted at Steve.

'Take notice of John will yeah for fuck's sake you can get yourself killed.'

Steve just shook his head in disagreement and shouted back to Jimmy,

'How can I let a thing like this go? Knowing what that poor kid is going through. I have already made a promise to the kid's mum and dad.'

'You've gone and what?' Jimmy shouted back at him. 'Don't you realise what you're getting yourself into?'

A slanging match kicked off between the two of them and it started to get out of hand. I positioned myself between Jimmy and Steve telling the two of them to take it easy and to calm themselves down, which they did.

Then for a couple of minutes, a gloomy silence descended on us all. In a way, I could understand Jimmy being concerned for Steve's welfare. After all he was his young nephew, the son of his sister, who he loved. Then again, I could also understand where Steve was coming from. He had a good strong principle, which I respected, and I knew if he had made a promise and given his word to the boy's parents, he would keep it - no matter what.

This was a terrible thing that had happened. It's hard to imagine that a gang of marauding scum could come onto the estate, in broad daylight, and kidnap a young kid. Something did have to be done about it, but what and how? So far the police were out of the question.   Their involvement would definitely have put the boy's life in danger.

This ordeal was now into its fourth day, and time, which was imperative, seemed to be dragging on. The local schools had been on a two-week holiday and the kids were getting ready to go back and start their new term. With that hanging in the balance it would only be a matter of time before the lid was blown on it all. If and when, that did happen, it might just have been too late.   Yeah, I could understand Steve wanting to rescue the kid, and the way I was feeling about it all, so did I!

It's funny how in such a brief moment of time, a man could make a split second decision, which could change the rest of this life. That is exactly what happened at the meeting we had on that Monday. I know I promised myself, together with family and friends, that I would not get involved with any more vigilante activities, but I am what I am. I couldn't go against the grain. Not now, and particularly with what my friends and I strongly believed in.... Justice! Justice for those who can't defend themselves against the lowlife scum that prey on them.

So, this is it. I am about to show my hand to everybody who is here at this meeting. I know Jimmy will be very upset, with what I am about to say, but what the fuck? Steve is determined to rescue the kid anyway, with or without me!

I started by telling Jimmy what my feelings and thoughts were about it all. I finished by telling him, I had decided to go along with Steve. Just as I had expected he would, he went ballistic.

'You what?' he said to me. 'Don't you realise what you're letting yourself into? Your two brothers will go mad when they hear what you're about to do, John. We have all bent over backwards to keep you on the straight and narrow, now look what's happening. You are going the right way to fuck everything up, not only for yourself John, but for Carol too!'

He carried on with his ranting and raving, shouting that we would all end up getting ourselves killed or doing a long time in jail. I tried my best to reason with him, which wasn't easy. However, I did eventually calm him down. I then told him, in a sarcastic manner, how surprised I was that he thought so positive of me. To soften the blow, I came up with a guarantee; Steve and the rest of our crew wouldn't come unstuck as long as I was dealing with the matter. I even went as far as telling him I would stake my life on it. He just sat there looking at me for a moment and seemed unconcerned about what I had just said. He stood up from where he was seated, saying he had heard enough. He then turned his back on the four of us, opened the front door of my apartment and went out closing it loudly behind him.

After Jimmy had left we all sat there looking at each other and shrugging. Young Steve seemed upset over it all.

'Your Uncle Jimmy is a good man really, Steve.' I told him. ' We could all see he was behaving a bit erratic here, but when you think about it, he was only trying to watch your back, so don't worry too much about it all.'

I went on to tell him that he would probably calm down and chill out about it later on, and when he did he would realise that the three of them were in good hands with me. I then suggested that the four of us should get to work immediately as time was now of the essence.

So it began, our planning, organising the best method of how to deal with this terrible situation.

HOW TO CATCH A TWO LEGGED RAT

The first thing that I stipulated on the agenda whilst we were discussing our plans was that it must be an absolute secret. It was imperative that nobody should know; not even the boy's parents. Secondly my aim was to find out as much as possible about the kidnappers. I began this by grilling Steve; I wanted to know everything he knew, no matter how trivial it may have seemed. I kept questioning and pressurising him about it all. He must have felt like he was being put through a strong interrogation by the police.

'Think hard Steve.' I said. 'What about the one who picks the money up from the shop each night? Do you have any more on that little rat?'

He then told me something I thought was very important; in fact it turned out to be absolutely essential. He could definitely identify the one who makes the pickup. This also had been supported by Carl and Chris, who themselves had been with Steve on three occasions when the pickup had taken place. I asked all three of them did they ever put a tail on the little rat when he came out of the shop. They said it was virtually impossible to follow him by car or on foot, the reason being, not only was it dark at that time but he comes and goes on a BMX pushbike. They said they did try to follow him a couple of times but they had always lost him. It seems once he comes out of the shop he peddles dead fast on his bike with the lights off, zigzagging down side streets and cutting through narrow alleyways. To me that is just typical of today's lowlife scum, they even have their own rat runs staked out... don't they? After I had listened carefully to what Steve and Carl had told me, particularly about the one on the bike, I had a pretty good idea of the best and fastest way of how to deal with this lot. I then started to outline my plan to the three of them, by first suggesting that we will cop for the rat who is on that bike. If we get him he will lead us to where they have the young kid holed up. Steve asked me. 'Do you mean we actually snatch him?'

'Yeah, we'll kidnap him and let's see how he likes it. We will bundle him into the van like we have done to the other scumbags in the past, and take him away somewhere'
Then Carl said to me.

'Will we be taking him outside of the shop John? You know it's a bit iffy there; someone might clock us grabbing him and everything.'

'Look,' I said. 'It doesn't matter whether we cop for him outside the shop or down the street, even if it means I have to knock him off his bike. One way or another we have got to get him and get him fast'

Carl wanted to know the ins and outs of everything; to which he was obviously entitled.

'What if we get him and he won't come across with anything? You know what I mean John, he might not grass on the rest of his scumbag mates, especially that Sick Mick fella; he might be too scared?'

'Let me tell the three of you something here and now. You all know the way I work, and you have all seen the way I perform, right? Once I get my hands on that rat I will guarantee to the three of you, that within five minutes of getting him, believe me, he will cough up alright. He will be only too glad to tell me. Yeah, let's see how he likes being kidnapped and tortured!'
I continued:

'What we will be going up against are not the average teenage lowlife scum, but older vicious bastards who are armed with guns. This then puts us all in a dangerous position regarding our safety. So when the time does come for us to take action, there will be no way I will be steaming into any of those animals with just a wooden pick-axe handle in my hand. I mean let's face it what chance has a piece of wood got against a bullet? Shooters are what we are going to be up against this time.'

I looked directly at the three of them sitting there listening to me, and I wondered what their reaction would be to what I am about to tell them next. I mean after all these three decent young men have never been in trouble in their lives. No police records, nothing, they are absolutely snow white!

So I gave it to them straight.

'I know what you all think about the use of guns, but this is dead serious and our lives could be in jeopardy. So for that reason we have to arm ourselves. By that I mean; not you three, I will be the one who will be carrying and I will be the one when the time does come; to steam into that rat hole. Let's have it right, what other alternative have we got?'

I paused and waited for a reply from them. Steve was the first to speak

'Whatever it takes John, I am with you all the way.'

Carl and Chris both nodded in agreement,

'Ok,' I said. 'Now that we've got that part sorted we can move on to the next part. Oh by the way, you will all have to wear vests (body armour), for when it does go off. I can get all that sorted by a good friend of mine, who will supply me with that gear and a shooter.'

I emphasised again to them that we have to move fast, as I wanted this all completed by tomorrow at the latest. I remember Steve saying to me.

'John, are you sure about that? I mean its Monday afternoon now.'

'Yeah I'm sure.' I told him, 'We have all said enough at this meeting, now let's start putting our words into action'

We were still plotting and planning on that Monday afternoon and I hadn't realised how quickly the time had gone by, it was almost four o'clock. We must have been talking none stop for nearly four hours.

Carol had arrived back after being on her long shopping trip, we quickly ceased the conversation of the plans we were about to carry out and I introduced her to Carl and Chris. She already knew who Steve was. Like the good lady Carol is, she quickly set about making tea and knocking up some sandwiches.

After ten minutes or so Carol asked if Kate the little dog had been out. I apologised to her saying we had been that busy trying to finish a business deal that I just hadn't had the time to take the dog for a walk. I told her we had finished our meeting and that Steve, Carl and Chris were going now. I decided to walk out with the three of them, and at the same time I would take the dog with me. After all, we had been sitting down for just over four hours. I suggested to them that it wouldn't be a bad idea if we all took a stroll along the city's waterfront. This, I thought, would be ideal to stretch our legs out a bit, and we could also finish tying up a few loose ends.

We had been walking for about twenty minutes or so and had now finalised our plans for later on. The four of us including the dog had stopped not too far from the Liver Buildings. I looked at one of the many clocks on this majestic building; it was showing the time was half past five. The city traffic had started to build up; it was a typical Monday evening rush hour with the hustle and bustle of people coming and going. I looked briefly at all this city life going on around me, and I thought to myself; God, I love this place, I would never leave here. This city is my home and it will always be in my blood, until the day I die. I am forever praising the beauty and good side of this city, yet quite a lot of people who live here would say that there is a darker side to it, I suppose in a way that is very true, especially where ruthless violence and crime is an everyday occurrence; which at the moment seems unstoppable. Anyway, enough of my philosophising it's back to the nitty-gritty, where we will try to sort this other fuckin' mess out.

Just before my three friends and I split, which was now six o'clock, we agreed that I would meet them on the Wood Green estate at ten o'clock that evening. We needed a place where we could take the rat on the bike after we had captured him. There are plenty of dilapidated run down houses on the estate, and after us having a further discussion Steve assured me there wouldn't be a problem; he could get one of the empty houses sorted out for the business. Now that we had all that part of the plan tied up, my next move was to make contact with a trusted friend of mine with regards to getting hold of a gun and some body armour. I will also need a motor, preferably a small van, which will obviously be down to nobody. The guy I will be dealing with is a friend I have known and trusted for years. My two brothers Frank and Paul know and respect him too. He is like ourselves, being from the old school, not like the other stupid pricks of today, who pass the parcel (gun) to one another after they have used it. For instance; tit-for-tat shootings on one another and other senseless and motiveless crimes. No wonder they come unstuck!

Guns are a modern disease these days, and gun crime is on the increase, there is no doubt about that, yet all these crimes committed with a fire-arm doesn't necessarily mean that the streets are full of guns like some of the media and the public make out. For example; that same gun could be used up to about twenty or thirty times by different individuals; hence the term pass the parcel (they lend the gun to one another). The police themselves know that this goes on amongst these shooters. I mean think about it; it's like me saying to someone can you get me or lend me a gun. Now supposing the gun that I have borrowed has been involved with other serious crimes including murder, would I be bothered? Would I fuck! This was simply because after I have finished with it, it would be handed back and then passed on to someone else to use.

This certainly won't be happening in my case. My friends and I are against using guns, but we are left now with no alternative. I mean don't get me wrong; I have used them in the past on certain heist or armed robberies we've done, but they were always used as a frightener; not to kill or hurt anybody. The sort of gun that we used all those years ago was a shotgun. The reason being it seemed to command respect; as looking down the barrel of a shotgun would terrify anybody! Now though, what we are up against, the weapons that most of this scum are using are handguns; which are mainly automatics. There will be no chance whatsoever of me using an automatic gun. No way! I will request from my friend a revolver, preferably a snub-nose revolver. The reason for this preference is; a revolver can never jam like an automatic. Even the American police force prefer a revolver to an automatic, because if it means life or death; meaning there is a stand-off - a gun pointed at you and your gun pointed at them - your gun isn't going to jam.

I had just four hours to get everything boxed –off, before going onto the Wood Green estate to meet up with Steve and co. I had made contact again with my friend about the parcel (gun and body armour) I was to pick up. He and I agreed to meet at 9.30pm. He explained to me that the van and goods would be parked on the driveway of a dead-safe house.

Now that I had heard everything was going according to plan; I thought I could spend the next hour in the company of Carol and at the same time get a bite to eat. I just couldn't bear the thought of Carol having any suspicions about what my friends and I were about to do.

On that fateful night; a night I will never forget, obviously I often think back on it and about how over-confident I was; me being the organiser, thinking I knew it all. Little did I realise what the outcome was going to be.

Another thing I remember and will not forget of that night, are my friend's last words to me; after me having got the van and other gear that was inside it off him, he said, 'be careful John, I mean you *are* carrying now, so be careful!'

I remembered one of my golden statements and one that I always adhered to; *very seldom would one man, on his own, get a pull by the bizzies*. The route I had taken to go to the Wood Green estate was a well-used, busy route; so less suspicious. I knew I couldn't afford to get a pull by the bizzies.

It was just on ten o-clock, as I was about to enter the estate I pulled up at a crossroads. Directly facing me was a police car with two bizzies in it. I put my indicator on to turn right. They obviously had priority to go before me, but unlike bizzies they used a bit of courtesy and let me go first. They probably thought I was just an ordinary working guy coming home from work. I thought 'that's very courteous of them letting me go. If only they knew. So far so good!'

I drove onto the Wood Green estate; the meet was just before the block of shops where that rat on the bike makes his pick-up. I decided to park the van in a side street next to the shops. On doing so I saw there were two businessmen in a car. One was leaning into the car talking to his colleague the other one looked at me, but I thought nothing of it. They looked like ordinary guys; they didn't bother me, my confidence was riding high.

Unfortunately, they were parked in the place where I was going to park. I decided to drive past them and park on the other side of the shops, but on doing so they drove away, but I thought I would just stay parked here. The reason I chose that spot was there was no one facing it and no one around. If we were going to capture him just there, that would be an ideal place to bundle him into the van. Unless of course we have to capture him somewhere else, but as I was thinking on that night, everything was going according to how I wanted it to go.

I alighted from the van. Obviously I had different clothes on now, disguised with glasses and a cap. I immediately made a phone call to Steve. He said they were sitting-off on the opposite side of the street in a motor, not far away from the shop where the action was going to take place.

'Ok,' I said to him. 'I'll pick the tools up and come over to the car.'

I went back to the van and took out a holdall, which contained the body armour and shooter, then walked to where Steve was parked with Chris. Carl was staying-put, by the shop. This was because if any suspicion arose he could mark our card. I got into the car with Steve and Chris, we started to drive to where the house was; the house that we will be using for the snatch; it was only a few streets away. I wanted to make sure it was suitable for what we wanted. Who knows, if this rat doesn't open up to us, we could be there a lot longer than we thought. When we *did* look at the chosen abode; it was in a row of dilapidated houses facing a derelict field; which I thought was ideal. There were a few kids hanging around as usual but we knew they would be gone by the time we did the business.

After I was satisfied about the house situation, I would say we had no more than 10 minutes before the rat on the bike showed himself. I quickly suggested we should all position ourselves by the shops immediately. To which we did, with each one of us selecting our own patch. By doing it this way we could all close in on the scumbag we are about to ambush, just in case he tries to do a runner.

Steve positioned himself more or less right outside of the premises. I myself stood outside a Chinese takeaway that was next door. It had a big menu on display in the window, which was ideal for me as it gave me a good reason to loiter; I could pretend to read the chip shop menu. I remember I was glancing around the area that night and it was fairly quiet, except for a few noisy kids hanging about. I looked at my watch and it was almost five minutes to ten; the Chinese takeaway had started to close. I knew we only had a few minutes to wait; that's of course *if* the rat on the bike turns up. All the time I had had my gloved hands in the pockets of my jacket. My right hand held the gun; it fitted snugly. The gun was exactly what I had ordered, a fully loaded 22 revolver, not too big and bulky.

Steve, who was still standing outside of the shop premises that belonged to the kidnapped boy's parents, was literally, only about five metres away to my right. The scum who live around here call it the 'Paki' shop, but they are so wrong. The bigots and the scum who call these people think they know it all; but they know fuck all. Mr and Mrs Khan, two decent, hard working people, are from India not Pakistan. Anyway, who they are or where they come from; does it really matter? The point is this; they are doing a good service for the community on this estate. I mean, let's face it; they both work from first thing in the morning until last thing at night. Are they really doing all this hard graft for themselves? I don't think so. I believe they are doing it to give their only son a decent life and upbringing. Can you imagine the turmoil that they are both going through? Hopefully though, that is all going to end very shortly.

It had started to go very quiet around here now and the kids who were hanging about had drifted away. I think with it being a Monday, like the other early week days, the evenings are always somehow quieter, the havoc and turmoil around this place usually goes on at the weekends. It is now just on eleven o-clock and the front window light of our shop had suddenly been switched off. This was better for us because it gave us a bit more cover. I glanced over at Steve and he nodded, I said, trying not to sound too loud,

'What do you think? Is he going to show or what?'

Steve sort of shrugged and said, 'he should have been here by now.'

'Ok,' I said. 'We will hang on a bit longer.'

I then turned and started to walk slowly in the opposite direction to Steve, again filling a little bit of time and not drawing too much attention to myself.

Just as I was about to start pacing away I heard a slight commotion coming from where Steve was. I quickly turned around and spotted a dark hooded figure on a bike; which had no lights on. It mounted the pavement in front of the shop. Steve had done exactly what I had done; he turned and was making out he was a passer-by by walking away. I then saw the rat for the first time. He parked his bike outside the dimly lit shop and entered. Steve then quickly spun around to face me on the opposite side of the premises. I beckoned him to come towards me; which was only a few paces. We were now facing each other. I asked Steve, 'is that definitely the rat, are you sure?'

'Yeah, it's him; it's him, one hundred percent!'

Then, out of nowhere Carl and Chris appeared!

I said to the three of them, 'the minute he comes back out grab the bastard as fast as we can!'

We then positioned ourselves; Carl and Chris were both at one side of the shop door, and Steve and myself at the other side. We were ready, and we waited, adrenaline pumping like mad. I cautiously peered though the corner of the shop window and I could see the rat inside. He was standing side-on talking and gesturing to the couple, Mr and Mrs Khan, who were the behind the shop counter. I couldn't hear or make out what he was saying to the couple, but I could plainly see he was pointing his finger at them and shaking his hand aggressively. It made my blood boil, and I said to Steve, who was standing behind me,

'The minute he comes out of this door he needs to be knocked right out!'

'That's no problem,' Steve said opening his jacket. Secreted there, was a wooden club-like baton.

'I'll whack him with this'
I nodded back to him and said, 'fuckin' brilliant!'

At one point I was contemplating us all taking the rat from inside of the shop, but then it would mean us all wearing masks. The reason why I knocked that idea back was because it would frighten the life out of Mr and Mrs Khan. After all, they are going through enough already. I was still watching him through the window when he suddenly turned to face the door. He stopped for a brief moment and turned his head back to Mr and Mrs Khan. Again he started to point his finger at them and shouted something back to them as he came towards the door. I said to Steve, 'here he comes. Get ready!'

He swaggered up to the front door and pulled it open. He only took a couple of steps outside when we pounced on him, pulling him down to the floor. I gave the nod to Steve and he whacked him with the club. He went spark out! I quickly looked around, 'so far so good;' there was nobody in sight. Even if there were, the people around here would not get involved. When something like this happens on these estates they all seem to turn a blind eye to what's going on. Chris, Steve and myself half carried and dragged the rat around the corner to where our van was parked. I asked Carl to bring the bike along too. We bungled the scumbag into the van, and Steve and Chris stayed in the back of it along with the rat. I was to drive. As the bike was too awkward to fit in the van I told Carl to follow us on it.

We pulled up outside of the dilapidated house, the one we had selected, which was only a couple of streets away. Steve got out of the van first and went to make the entrance. The windows and doors of these run down houses had all been boarded up with corrugated sheets of metal, but because of the vandalism around here most of them had been ripped off. Carl who had been following us on the bike had arrived. I asked him if everything was alright and had anybody seen anything of what we had just done, as I wouldn't like anything to come on top for us at this stage. He said everything was dead sound. It was always the police I was concerned about when doing anything like this, but then thinking about them, they wouldn't be around these 'no go areas' anyway. Steve had made the entrance via the front door.

'Let's get this fuckin' rat inside!'

He was still dazed and mumbling when we dragged him from the back of the van. Once we were all inside we placed the rat on the floor in the centre of the room. I then told everybody to put their ballies (masks) on. Steve had a small torch in his hand.

I noticed the lowlife was starting to come round. I began opening our tool bag that I had fetched from the van. I pulled out a more powerful torch light from it, which I brought because I knew there would be no electrics on in any of these run down properties. I switched the torch on and it lit up the room of the house. The place was in a right mess; discarded rubbish and other pieces of junk were lying around everywhere.

I managed to prop the torch on a broken wall shelf. All of us were now standing in a sort of a circle fully masked, looking down on the lowlife scum. He was now in a sitting position in the centre of the filthy floor. He started whimpering, rubbing his head at the same time. From the moment we had snatched him from the shop until now had taken less then five minutes. I crouched slowly down to him wearing my black

243

mask. I knew by looking at him he had quickly gathered his senses, as he looked absolutely terrified. I needed to extract information out of this prick as fast as possible as the other rats; his associates, the ones who are holding the kid somewhere, are waiting for him to return with the pickup money, and I think I know how this scum works; if he doesn't return on time to them with the money, they will know something is wrong and will make contact with him on his mobile. Time was definitely running out for us. So I began talking to him slowly and menacingly, 'listen carefully to me cunt. You know why you're here don't yeah?'

He mumbled something like, 'er no'. He then pulled an envelope from his jacket pocket.

'Here it is.'

His shaking hand passed the envelope to me. I took it off him and looked at the money, there was about two or three hundred quid in it. This was the hard earned money that the boy's parents had slogged their guts out for.

'We're not interested in the fuckin' money you prick, and whilst I'm at it, give me your phone.'

He quickly passed me his mobile phone. I knew this could ring at any moment now from the other scumbags. I had to put the real frighteners on him fast.

Whilst I was still crouching over him, I looked up at Steve and Carl; I told the two of them to turn this rat on his back and pin him down. They quickly pinned his arms down. By now he was really trembling with fright and looking up at me. I then pulled a small glass bottle out of my jacket; it was filled with powerful, smouldering acid. I had secretly acquired this earlier on that day. The room was deadly quiet. I opened the bottle just above his face and said to him, 'you know what this is don't ya?'

He was now petrified, and sounding hysterical he squealed, 'don't! Don't do it mate. Please mate, I'm...'

Steve and Carl looked at me, and I could tell by their eyes they were both shocked at what I was about to do. I went off my head a bit and screamed at him.

'This acid is going right in your fuckin' eyes if you don't tell us where that Sick Mick has that young kid. Do you fuckin' hear me? Hey?'

I screamed again at him, 'tell me now, or I will fuckin' blind ya!'

He cracked straight away, 'ok, ok hang on mate, but honest to God, honest to God, I had nothing to do with it. I'm only the run about.'
'Who do you think you're fuckin' kidding? I don't give a fuck what you are. You better tell us the fuckin' truth. Now!'

We called him the rat on the bike, and do you know what? It is so weird, but he actually resembled one. He had pointed features, sticking out ears and his two front teeth protruded like a rodent's. He was a rat alright.....a two legged one!

I knew by using the powerful psychological method that I did on him, he would roll over. His loyalty to the rest of his scum gang had gone right out of the window. I extracted that information in just over two minutes; he told us everything from start to finish. I was not surprised at all when he revealed to me the whereabouts the kidnapped boy was being held. It was very local and not too far away; in another dilapidated house just like this one. The house was situated in the centre of a block of others, on the far side of *this* estate. I always had the feeling that those rats would be holding the kid somewhere around these parts.

I went on to glean every bit of information out of this scumbag. When he had told me what I wanted to hear, my number one priority was to get him to make a phone call to his perverted friend 'Sick Mick'. We were all now standing in a circle and looking down at this pathetic, whimpering bag of shit that was still sitting in the centre of the floor. I slowly crouched down to him again; only this time I had the fully loaded shooter in my hand. I grabbed him by his throat and I forced the barrel of the gun into his mouth, I wanted him to believe I was going to shoot him there and then. He quite obviously thought that the info he had given to us was enough, and that he was of no further use to me. This was, of course, all part of the psycho I was using on him before he made the phone call. I pulled the gun barrel out of his mouth; he was gasping for breath and shivering. Let's not forget; that all the time I was tormenting him the room was deadly quiet, not one word had been spoken by my friends, who by the way looked very intimidating, all standing there in complete silence. This time I put the gun barrel between his eyes and at the same time I began talking to him.

'You are gonna make a call to that sick cunt of a mate of yours, are you listening to me?'

He nodded his head trembling and said, 'yeah, I am yeah.'

'What I want you to say to that sick bastard is what I tell you to say to him, and not another word. Got it?'

He mumbled, 'yeah.'

I know how these scumbags work and what they get up to when they are on the blower to one another. They all have their own secret little passwords to each other if anything has come on top for them. So I told him, 'one word out of place or any slip-ups and I will put a bullet right in your fuckin' head.'

'I won't, I won't.' he replied, 'Honest to God I won't!'

I knew that his arse had completely gone, and he would do exactly what I instructed him to do. I started to brief him; I told him to tell the 'Sick Mick' scumbag that the boy's parents have just pulled up five grand, and that they are going to pull the other five grand up tomorrow, but they want a guarantee that their son will be released. I warned him he must play the part well on the phone, and if he makes one false move I will shoot him dead. I passed him back his mobile phone and I got Steve to crouch down next to him, to listen in on the call. I then held the gun to his head and told him he had better pull this off.

'Now make that fuckin' call!'

He made the call, and it went something like this:

The Rat:	'Alright Mick?'
Sick Mick:	'Yeah. Where the fuck are you?'
The Rat:	'Mate, you're not gonna believe this, I've just copped for five grand off the two Pakis.'
Sick Mick:	'You what? How? What's going on?'
The Rat:	'Stop getting para' (paranoid) will you. I told you I've got the fuckin' readies here, here on me now. That's why I'm a bit late getting back.'
Sick Mick:	'Aw, fuckin' hell, I'm made up. Hurry up and get over here with it.'

The Rat:	'Yeah ok, but listen to the rest. The silly Paki cunts are pulling another five grand up for us tomorrow; they want the kid back though.'
Sick Mick:	'Fuckin' brilliant.'

Sick Mick could be heard talking to someone else who was in the rat-hole with him. He was saying something like, 'Yeah, he's got the readies with him. Yeah, you heard five grand.'

The Rat:	'Hey Mick, who's in there with ya? Who's that you're talking to?'
Sick Mick:	'It's only Tomo you soft cunt. Just hurry up and get over here with the readies.'
The Rat:	'Yeah alright. I'm just telling the two Pakis the score. Then I'll be over to see you, but don't forget Mick; we have to give them their kid back.'
Sick Mick:	(laughing) 'Oh I don't know about that one. (Still laughing) 'I'll have to think about that.' (Laughter)

The phone conversation between the two lowlife scumbag's had ended. I asked the rat about the boy's welfare and how had he been bearing up, particularly with that perverted bastard called 'Sick Mick'. He answered me rather sheepishly and put his head down; he admitted to me that the boy had been getting violently and sexually abused. After he had revealed this to me and my friends, who themselves were shocked at hearing it, Steve started pacing up and down and growling, it had really upset him.

I couldn't quite make my mind up at this stage in the mission, the problem was did I take this lowlife with us, or did I leave him behind with one of our crew. After careful consideration, I thought; fuck it, the prick is coming with us, after all, *he* is the one who knows the way into the place.

According to his information, the house where they had the boy was situated in a block of terraced houses, being the second to last of the dilapidated row. Every door and window on these properties was all boarded up with sheets of metal, with the acceptance of the first house, the back door on this house had been forcibly opened, and that back door was the way in. Once we were inside it was a matter of climbing the stairs and going through an open access in the bedroom ceiling, which lead into the loft. Inside the loft there was a divided, thin, lightweight, breezeblock wall.

The centre of that wall had been smashed-in; leaving a large gaping hole that lead into the adjoining property. This was the property where the young kid was being held, and according to what the rat had told us, they had him held downstairs in the front living room of the place. There was one more slight problem; a small window in the front bedroom of the place had been forced open, this of course was used as a look out. We had to be very careful about this. The Sick Mick fella and his gang of scum could observe anything from that window, coming or going in the street below. It looked like these scumbags had everything boxed off for themselves; having their own rat-run and rat-holes, together with an escape route.

When we were told about this 'den of iniquity', which incidentally was on the far side of the estate, Steve and I drove around there to suss the place out. The time was ticking away by now, it was coming up to half past eleven, and I wanted all this to be over-with by twelve-o-clock. So we all got our heads together and had our final brief. I instructed everybody to put their vests on, (bullet-proof body armour), not that they really needed to wear them, after all, I was the one who would be going in on this and it would be me and only me who would be carrying the baby (small hand gun). Precautions have to be taken really seriously on something as heavy as this though. I mean who knows a big shooting match could kick-off.

After we had sorted everything out amongst ourselves, I spoke to the rat who was still sitting on the floor in the middle of the room.

'Listen you, you're the one who is going to get me into that fuckin' house one way or another, do you hear me?'

'Yeah, yeah ok.' he said.

'Remember this,' I warned him. 'I will be right behind you all the time and if you try to warn them or anything, you will be the first to get this.' I said showing him the gun. 'Right in your fuckin' head. Remember I don't give a fuck about you; you're nothing to me. So any slip-ups out of you and I will fuckin' kill you. Alright?'

'I'll go along with it mate, I know the score.' Then the cheeky bastard said to me.

'Are yeah gonna let me go when all this is sorted?'

I just ignored what he had asked me, and I told Carl and Chris to get this prick in the van. They both began to drag him up from the floor. Steve had gone to fetch the van from where we had parked it earlier on. He was going to do the driving.

He came back into the house a few minutes later. I asked him if everything was alright out there; meaning nothing suspicious looking or anything.

'Yeah.' he said. 'No problems, the motor is outside.'

'Ok,' I said. 'Let's all fuck off around there and get this done.'

With that, we all piled into the van. Chris and Carl with the rat in the back. I sat in the front with Steve. He switched the motor on, and we pulled away, heading towards our destination.

THE RATS' NEST

Surprisingly, the place where the scum were holed-up with the boy was only five minutes away. My adrenaline was starting to pump; things were going through my mind fast on that short journey. Like a fine toothcomb, I was going over everything that the rat had told me about earlier on. Firstly, the Sick Mick fella definitely had a gun. The other one called Tomo who was now with him, I was not sure about. Even the rat who I had been grilling right up until the last minute wasn't too sure whether Tomo had a gun. There were two more scumbags in their gang, but according to what the rat had told me, they hadn't been around the place for a few days. I was just hoping that when I did steam in; those other two wouldn't be there. Otherwise, I could have had a big problem on my hands. Anyway, that's a chance I just had to take, as there was no going back now.

Although the drive to the place was only five minutes away, to me it seemed to be taking a lot longer. Not one word had been spoken amongst any of us along the way. I glanced around as we were driving along this part of this council estate, it resembled a ghost town, and everywhere seemed deserted. Most of the houses were empty and vandalised; some had no roof on them. The place was very dark around there; being that there were no streetlights on. This is the part of the estate where some of the lowest of the lowlifes live and hang out. Even the bizzies don't go there; it is a *no go area*.

Steve suddenly pulled up the van. 'John,' he said. 'The place is in the next street.'

'Right,' I said. 'That's ok. We will park the van here and go the rest of the way on foot. But before we do I want him,' I said pointing to the rat in the back of the van. 'To make a call to that Mick fella.'

I asked Carl to get into the front of the van while I jumped in the back. I told the rat exactly what to say when he made the phone call. He was to make out he seemed excited, telling the Mick fella he had got the money with him and also had some nice Charlie (coke) on him. I told the rat to make it all sound good and to pump him in a round-about-way, as to whether the other two scumbags were there with him. Finally, I passed him a small plastic bag, this I had found in the dilapidated house where we had just come from. I had put some folded newspaper inside it to make it look like a little parcel. I then told him, dead serious and looking menacing, that it would be me and him who were going into that place and into that loft, and that these three were going to stay behind in the house next-door. When we did get through to the other loft; before he dropped down through it, I wanted him to seem excited and to show the lowlifes the bag, making something up to them like saying, 'here it is' and wave the bag, before he dropped into the upstairs room. I was telling him to do this as a precaution, because I had a strong feeling that one of them might come up the stairs from the front room to meet him.

'You did say that they were operating in the front room downstairs didn't you?'

He looked at me really scared and said, 'yeah that's right, that's where it's all happening.'

'It had better be right for your sake, because you will be the first one to get it. Right? Now make the fuckin' call and tell him you will only be a few minutes. And I'm warning you now, really convince that sick bastard.'

He made a second call, and it was relayed like this:

The Rat:	'Alright Mick?'
Sick Mick:	'Yeah, what's happening?'
The Rat:	'I'm only a few minutes away.'
Sick Mick:	'What's the fuckin' hold up? You should have been here by now.'
The Rat:	'I know mate but I had to count the fuckin' readies didn't I? And listen (sounding excited) I had a touch for some boss charlie for us.'
Sick Mick:	'You what? I hope you're not fuckin' about with the money.'

The Rat:	'For fuck's sake stop panicking will you, it's good beak, and the readies are here with me. What's wrong with you? Oh by the way, are the other two there? You know Mick, the readies we've got and everything, I mean it was you, me and Tomo who sorted this business out, not the other two.'
Sick Mick:	(sounding like a growl) 'They're not here anyway, leave that to me. I'll sort the other two out.'
The Rat:	'Alright mate. Be there in a few minutes.'

The Rat had played his part very well, but then, wouldn't anybody if a gun was pointed at your head, ready to blow the fuckin' brains out of you.

When we all listened to the way the rat performed on his phone, I thought it would certainly have convinced me. I asked Steve, 'do you think that perverted, sick scumbag has fallen for what's been said?'

'Dead right he has,' he replied. Carl and Chris agreed too.

We all got out of the van making sure we closed the doors very quietly and crossed over to the street where the row of houses were. I was in the lead and the rat was following behind me, we were all walking in single file, masked up. I took a glance around at everybody; the scene looked like what you would see in a movie, a team of SAS men going on a raid mission. The only difference was; we were not the SAS, and this wasn't a movie. This was real, we were vigilantes who were disciplined and determined!

We had entered the street where our target was, there were no streetlights on and the night was pitch black now. I looked up at the sky, there wasn't even moonlight. This of course was ideal as it gave us all a good cover. We still had to be very careful though, not to get ourselves exposed. I stopped walking and so did the others. Ahead, not 100 yards away at the most, was the row of dilapidated houses. They were situated on the right side of the street, the same side we were on. The first house on the block was the one we would be entering via the back door; its gable end was facing us. I suggested that from now on we should all move over to the far side of the street and approach it from the back, because there was no other way we could take it. I just got another one of those instincts of mine, and I could visualise that sick psycho peering through the front bedroom window, looking out excited, waiting to see the rat return with the money.

It's been so far so good and I wouldn't want anything to come on top now that we have got this far. We carried on. With it being so dark we were stumbling at times, trying our best to tread carefully over some of the rubbish and debris that was scattered about. We finally approached the back of the first house and I myself was the first in, followed by the rat. It was deadly quiet inside the place, but then I heard music being played, I told everybody to keep quiet for a second and listened intently. It *was* music being played, and it was coming from next door, the very house where those scumbags had the kid.

I whispered to Steve, Carl and Chris, 'I want you three to stay put here just in case.'

They all nodded, but Steve was insisting on coming in with me. I wouldn't have any of it and I told him straight, that if a big shooting match goes off I want him and the rest to fuck off as fast as they could. I showed him my gun and said,

'I'm not carrying this for fuck all, it will be either them or me.'

I growled a little at the three of them and said, 'that's the way it has to be, it's my way or no way!'

Young Steve was still a bit reluctant but he finally relented and agreed with me. Just before the rat and I went up the stairs, my last words to the three of them were, if I do come unstuck, it's better for one of us to get it than the four of us.'

I turned away from them, and with the gun in my hand I said to the rat, 'come on you, get in front of me and lead the way.'

We both started to climb the stairs.

I began climbing those stairs very cautiously and thinking to myself, 'I just hope to God that the Mick fella is not hiding and waiting for us somewhere in the adjoining loft,' but when we got to the top, so far it seemed ok. The rat and I were now standing on the stairs landing, and I could see the loft above us, it had an aluminium ladder leading up to it. It was fairly dark up there and if there was going to be an ambush on me I thought; it will happen when I reach the inside of that loft.

As I was feeling and thinking this way my adrenaline was pumping like mad and the music coming from inside the place was playing slightly louder. I looked at the rat and motioned to him with the gun to start climbing the aluminium ladder. He went up a couple of rungs on it and it started to creak. I thought 'fuck I wish that music was louder'. Then suddenly, as luck would have it, a loud noise started to come from above, it was getting louder and nearer. At first I thought it was a plane but then I realised it was a helicopter passing by.

I grabbed at this opportunity as it enabled us to disguise any noise we might make climbing the ladder. I told the rat to hurry and get up the ladder; he did so with me right behind him like a shot. As the helicopter was literally passing over the house we both were standing motionless in the loft. We listened as the sound starting to get fainter and fainter as it passed over on its way. It is not unusual these days to hear a police helicopter now and again passing over these lawless ghettos, sometimes they are chasing car hijackers or on the lookout for skunk factories. My heart was beating faster now, and because the place was fairly dark I could just about see the breezeblock wall with the smashed-in gaping hole. It was now just a matter of us passing through it and we would be in the house next door.

The rat on my instructions went through it first, with me right behind him. When I entered I looked down onto the floor where I could see light coming up from the open loft hatch. I could also hear the music, the same music from before, only now I could hear it slightly louder.

I got myself closer to the rat and I whispered to him, 'I want you to look through that hatch in the loft floor, just put your head through it and if nobody is there raise one arm up to me, if there is somebody there, whoever it is, start talking to him and get him to go down the stairs into the front room with you.'

He crouched down onto his knees and put his head more or less through the open hatch. He got back up and nodded to me that nobody was there. I told him to stand away from it whilst I had a look, I could see we were above the stairs landing and there was a wooden table directly below us; this was their way in and out of loft. I also saw a dim ray of light coming from the room down the stairs and could hear the music still being played. I quickly pulled my head back up. I was excited now; all my body seemed as if it had had a massive powerful energy pumped through it.

I spoke to the rat in a growling sort of a whisper, 'right, get your head back through there, I want you to shout for that fuckin' Sick Mick bastard, make out to him you are dead excited, then show him the plastic bag, wave it to him, the soft cunt will think it's full of readies! Then drop down onto that table below and run down the stairs to him with the bag, try and get him into the front room with you. Alright?'

'Yeah alright, alright!'

'Remember, if you fuck up you will be the first one to get this,' I said thrusting the shooter in his face.

'I'll do it, I'll do it,' he replied hurriedly.

Again I whispered slowly to him, 'listen, once I get that kid out of there and sort that Sick Mick bastard out, I will let you fuck off. Alright?

But if you fuck up... I will kill you!'

'Yeah ok, ok.' he said.

'Now go on, get over to that hole and start your performing.'

263

I stood directly in front of him as he crouched down to the open hatch in the floor. He looked up at me for a moment; I pointed the gun at his head and nodded indicating for him to do his fuckin' acting routine.

He quickly put his head through the open hatch and shouted in an excited voice, 'Mick, Mick!!'

The volume of the music coming from down the stairs suddenly turned lower, I then heard a bit of a commotion like a sort of a scrambling of feet, then a voice.

'Now then, where the fuck have ya been?'

'I've been shouting ya for ages, you mustn't have heard me.'

'I've been up there looking out the window and waiting for ya.'

'Well I didn't see ya.'

'Yeah well, a fuckin' bizzie chopper flew past, and we had to come back down. Didn't we Tomo? Didn't you hear it?'

'Yeah I was just coming in when that chopper came over. Anyway fuck all that just look what I've got.'

He started laughing and flashed the plastic bag to them. Obviously I couldn't see their reactions or what was going on. The rat pulled his head back in from the hatch gave me a quick look and still clutching the bag dropped down onto the table below, I heard him go down the stairs fast so I took a chance and sneaked a look, I just about saw the back of him at the bottom of the stairs, and could see the body of somebody else by the dim light coming from the front room. I heard the rat shouting in an excited voice.

'Get us a can will ya.' (Meaning lager or beer).

I knew every second was vital to me now. I could visualise what would be going on in that front room, particularly where the plastic bag was concerned. I had deliberately tied that bag in to several really tight knots, knowing full well it would be difficult and awkward for anybody to open. I had done this to buy me some time, vital time, I have to act fast here I only have seconds left. I immediately sprung into action; I dropped myself down from the loft onto the table below, fuck the noise now, I don't want to be confronting that Sick Mick with a shooter in his hands. I was down those stairs in two to three seconds at the most. The room door was wide open when I stepped into it. It was lit up by torch-lights. I stood there ballied up with the gun in my hand. I heard one of them speak.

'What the fucks going....?'

In the centre of the room two men were standing together, one of them had his back to me; the other who was facing me looked very surprised. To describe him; he was on the slim side about five foot ten inches tall, aged mid

265

twenty's, with a gaunt looking face and sunken eyes. The one who had his back to me was a big juiced up type a typical skin head, the back of his neck was thick and fat with a tattoo across it. I spoke to the pair of them.

'Don't you fuckin' pair of twats move, or I will put this right in your fuckin' heads.'

The one with his back to me slowly turned around, he was holding the plastic bag, his face was fatty and evil looking. I would say he too was about mid twenty's. I shouted to him.

'I told you not to fuckin' move didn't I?'
He gave me an evil grin; he was holding the bag up and said to me,

'Is this what you've fuckin' come for? You Paki's are all the fuckin' same. Ya give it in one hand and take it out with the other'

Now because I was masked and gloved up the evil bastard thought I was an Asian and was after the so-called £5,000. It's quite obvious they had not yet got the bag quite open when I burst in on them.

Whilst this was going on I caught a movement to the left of them it was the rat, he was at the far side sitting down on something, I don't know whether it was a chair or a box.

'I think you have got me all wrong haven't you? You perverted cunt!'

'Alright take the fuckin' readies.' He threw over the bag. 'Just fuck off out of here and we'll call it quits.'

'Now you listen to me you fuckin' beast. You make one more fuckin' move and I will put one right in you.'

He got arrogant, and silly with it, he started growling and snarling at me.

'You haven't got the fuckin' arse to use that. And you know what? I bet it's a phoney.'

He then made a mistake; he took a step towards me. I lowered the gun and fired it directly at his groin, hoping it would blow his dick off! He went down on the floor screaming and holding his crotch. I watched him wriggle in agony. Then I caught the other scumbag Tomo leaning over to pick something up from a small table. It was a gun!

He raised it and screamed something at me, but my reflex action was too quick, I shot him in the stomach. He too went down. I pounced on him taking away the shooter, he was moaning on the floor holding his stomach, pumping with blood. There was no way that pair of scum were going anywhere in a hurry!

A SHOCKING DISCOVERY

'Where have they got the kid?' I shouted to the rat; who by now was cowering,

He jumped up and went to the far right corner of the room where an old wooden curtain pole about five foot long was fixed across the corner. It had some dark shabby looking cloth draping on it as a makeshift curtain. The rat pulled the lower part of it about two foot up from the floor, and holding it in his hand he said to me in a false, friendly voice, 'here he is, here. I've found him!'

I went over, and peered underneath the curtain; what I found sickened me to the core. The poor kid was naked, lying face down on an old filthy mattress with both his hands tied behind his back. There were two powerful stand-up torches in this front room; the nearest one was on a chair. From what I could see of him he looked like his poor little body was battered and bruised, he was covered in what looked to me like bite marks. There was no doubt about it, the kid had been violently and sexually abused by that psychopathic paedophile, who was now lying there on the floor, moaning about his gunshot wound.

I was fuckin' angry and upset at the same time. I ripped the curtain and the pole off the wall and I screamed at the rat.

'Get me something to untie him with and fuckin' hurry up.'

I quickly took off my jacket and covered the lower part of the kid's body. With a look of terror on his face he turned to look at me. I started to speak to him softly, 'Amir, Amir!'

He looked at me, then I realised I still had my mask on, so I ripped it off.

'I'm a friend of your Mum and Dad.'

Just as I was trying to get the kid comfortable I caught a move at the far side of the room. One of the injured scumbags had made it to the door. It was the pervert Sick Mick, I leapt across the room at him. He was crouched over still holding his crotch in pain. He was bleeding heavily now. I pulled him back down onto the floor and smacked him across the fuckin' face with the gun and said to him, 'you're not going anywhere you fuckin' beast.'

Now the rat started to get fidgety, so I told him,

'Don't you fuckin' think of trying anything, or you will end up like those two.'

He sat down with his head in his hands and kept quiet. I went straight back to the boy. His hands were bound with like a leather thong. I shouted to the rat, 'did you find anything to untie him?'

'Here,' he said. 'This is all I've got.'
He handed me a small bladed knife. I took it from him and started to cut the leather thong away from the boy's wrists.

'Don't worry,' I told him. 'I'll have you out of here shortly.'

He started to rub his wrists when I cut him free and I noticed one of his hands had a sock over it. It was the hand with the severed finger. I asked where his clothes were. He then started talking. He said to me,

'My jeans are under this mattress with the rest of my clothes.'

'Do you want my help to get dressed?'

He replied politely and timidly, 'I can manage thank you.'

I spoke softly to him. 'I'm going to give you my mobile, and you can phone your Mum and Dad to tell them you are safe now and coming home in a few minutes.'

Just then I heard a noise that sounded familiar to me. The sound was getting louder as it was getting nearer. I then realised what it was. It was the police helicopter that had passed by ten minutes earlier. Only this time it didn't pass by. It hovered above this house...but why?

I instantly shot right out of the room, up the stairs and made my way to the front bedroom, which they had used as their look out. I approached the window very cautiously and peered out. The searchlight from the helicopter above was all over the house. Keeping my head well back from the window I glanced up and down the street... my heart sank; Police cars with lights flashing and their sirens screaming were coming towards this block from both directions. They were all screeching to a halt right outside the house. On my last glance I could see armed bizzies getting out of the cars. I just couldn't believe this was happening and I knew what to expect next.

I came away from the look out and climbed onto the table that was positioned underneath the loft hatch. I pulled myself up into the loft and went quickly through the hole in the dividing wall and into the loft next door. I put my head through and shouted for Steve. I shouted a couple of times but there was no answer. They all must have sussed this coming on and got themselves out of the way. I just hoped the three of them had made it.

I knew now I was fucked, there was no chance for me. The place was completely surrounded. I quickly went back to the front living room. There I could hear all the racket of the bizzies and the goings on outside. They were probably getting themselves prepared for a big stand off!

I asked the young boy, Amir, was he feeling ok and had he spoken to his mum. He told me he had spoken to his parents, but not realising, he had only gone and told his parents where he was! They will now more than likely be outside of here with the rest of the crowd that had been gathering.

I took a look around at this hellhole of a place; the two scumbags that I had shot were now in a bad way. They were both groaning and lying on the floor in their own blood, which seemed to be spreading everywhere. I had to get Amir out of here. I started to explain to him what I intended to do. First I asked if he was alright and could he walk ok? I mean afterall, the poor kid had been in this rat-hole for over three days and nights, and God only knows what he had gone through at the hands of that depraved, evil bastard who was now lying there on the floor.

He told me; trying to be brave, that he could walk ok. Then I assured him I would show him the way out of here. As I went on explaining the plan to the kid, I noticed that the rat was starting to pace around, and he looked sort of relieved. At one point he interrupted me when I was talking to the boy,

'There's no worries; I'll go out the back door with him.' The rat said to me, smiling.

I thought to myself that what the rat had just said seemed to make sense. Then I looked at Amir to ask him if that would be ok with him? I mean there was no way I could show myself out there, not yet anyway. Amir looked at the rat and then back at me, his body shook, he put his head down and stood there silent for a moment. I asked him what was wrong. He looked up at me and said.

'I don't want him to take him out of here.' He said pointing at the rat.

When I asked him why, he revealed to me what had really been going on, and what they had been doing to him during his capture. The kid began to pour his heart out to me. It turned out that not only had that sick paedophile Mick been at it with him, but so too had the rat...the fuckin' beast!

When the kid was telling me all of this, the rat kept trying to interrupt, blaming it on Sick Mick and making excuses that it wasn't his fault.

'I only went along with it.' He said to me. But if the truth be known; both of these lowlife beasts were raping the young kid on a regular basis. I turned and looked with a violent hatred towards this inhuman scumbag. I couldn't control myself, don't ask me why but I just lost it. I shot him there and then, the bullet caught him right between his legs. He too went down on the floor screaming in agony. Right after that shot rang out I heard my name being called. It was coming from outside.... *John Christian, John Christian!*

It was the bizzies on the megaphone. The helicopter was now circling around the house.

I looked at Amir after I had shot the rat and said to him,

'I didn't want you to see this Amir, but I just lost it with that scumbag.'

Funny at that moment, the kid didn't look shocked or anything. In fact he seemed pleased, but he didn't reply. I pointed to the scum on the floor.

'See these three beasts?' I said to him. 'If they got sent to jail for what they have done to you, do you know what? They would all be set free in a couple of year's time. Set free maybe to do it again to another kid.'

He just looked at me as if relieved.

'Ah come on kid,' I said. 'Let's go!'

We both ran up the stairs to the front room. The loudspeakers kept repeating my name, telling me to come out. I heard noise coming from next-door, it was them, the bizzies; the armed response team. It will only be minutes before they discover that dividing breezeblock wall with the hole in it. All kinds of noises seemed to be going on and getting louder by the minute. It felt like the whole house was shaking with the vibration and erratic noise from the helicopter as it now circled above the place. The loud speakers somehow seemed louder as they kept repeating my name.

'How the fuck do they expect me to communicate with them while all this racket is going on?'

There was only one thing for it; I had to make contact with the bizzies that were in the house next door. Amir was standing looking bewildered with all this commotion. I think he really needed medical treatment.

I explained to him, 'I will tell the police that you are coming through to them. Will that be ok Amir? You will be with your Mum and Dad in a few minutes. Ok mate?'

The poor kid managed a little smile to me and said, 'thank you.'

I got back onto the table and by standing on my tiptoes I could put my head through the hatch and could see into the loft. There were lights shining inside it. I looked across at the dividing breezeblock wall with the hole smashed in. A bizzie was looking right through it with a torch in his hand! In that instant we both saw each other, there was only about four or five metres between us. We both froze at seeing each other. I couldn't say for sure if he had a gun on him, but I know I still had mine on me. Anyway, now that we were fronting one another up I started to talk to him. I began by saying, 'I'm John Christian, tell the other police who are on the speakers that I will come to the front window and talk to them there.'

He didn't reply, he just stared at me. I carried on, 'I can't hear anything from inside here, the noise out of that chopper is drowning everything out.'

He still didn't answer; he just kept staring at me. I got a bit annoyed with him. 'Are you taking any notice of what I'm saying to you?'

He then shouted at me, 'You come out of there and lie down on that floor with both your hands stretched out.'

I couldn't believe what he was saying to me. Afterall, I'm only here to rescue the kid. I had a feeling now that he was armed. I saw a movement directly behind him, it was another bizzie. I knew now that they were definitely the armed response. I thought to myself, I had better reason with them, so I said to them both,

'Let's be sensible here. There is a young boy in here who was kidnapped and tortured for three fuckin' days, and he needs medical attention right away. He is going to come up through this hatch right now.'

I shouted down to Amir. 'Get up on this table next to me.'

At the same time I was still keeping my eyes on the armed police. I just had a feeling they would try to rush over to me. Amir got himself up onto the table and stood at the side of me. I quickly took my head down from the hatch and lifted Amir up. I started to push him through.

'Go on kid, you'll be ok now.'

I put my head back through the hatch and said to the police, 'this is the young kid who was kidnapped.'

I then reassured Amir as he walked slowly towards the police. I watched him go to the hole where the policeman was, and they helped him through. I shouted to them,

'There's three men in here and there's guns. I want you to tell your negotiator who keeps shouting out my name, I will go to the front window of this room in ten minutes, and please don't get any silly ideas about coming into this loft!'

They didn't answer me. So I shouted again,

'Remember, ten minutes, I'll be at that front window!'

MY MOMENT OF MADNESS

I jumped down from the table then I ran back down the stairs and into the front room. The rat was holding his lower parts and moaning in agony. He was in the corner of the room; he asked me if I would get him an ambulance, he was breathing heavily. He said he was going to die if he didn't get help. I told him to fuck off and took no further notice of him. The other scumbag Tomo was lying on the other side of the room underneath the front window. He was just lay there saying nothing. Sick Mick was sitting propped up against the wall with his head bowed. He obviously couldn't walk; he was bleeding heavily too. He lifted his head up when I entered the room. His fat evil face looked right at me then he kicked off trying to insult me,

'You're fucked now. Those bizzies out there have got the place surrounded and I'm fuckin' glad.' He tried to laugh. 'When they steam in here you'll be going down for a long, long time.'

'Oh will I now? ' I said to him.

'Yeah, I'm gonna make sure. When we all get out of here, me, Tomo and Billy,' (Billy was the rat's name which I didn't know until now). 'We will tell the bizzies how you shot all three of us.'

'Oh I see, now you're all going to conspire and give evidence against me in court.'

'Fuckin' too right we are'

'What about the young boy that you and that cunt over there kidnapped, tortured and raped?'

The evil bastard blanked out what I had just said to him, but he answered back to me.

'I see you've got your ballie off. I can I.D. you now, can't I?' He laughed again. 'I'm gonna say you was in on it with us, and the three of us can identify you.' Again he started to laugh. 'We'll put the finger on you.' His laugh became really evil.

I looked at these lowlife degenerates and thought to myself, who was the worst one out of the three? Or are they all as bad as each other?' Here we have the lowest form a human being can be; callous, remorseless scum, lacking in empathy, who don't have the ability to form emotional relationships with others. These lowlifes function without a conscience.

I am aware I will be sent to prison for shooting these three evil beasts, and I also know the sentence I will receive will be life…. and I mean life. I will never be set free again. Yet on the other hand, these lowlife scumbags will only get a fraction of my sentence when they go down for the crimes they committed on that young boy. They will most probably only serve a couple of years each at the most. To me that's not justice!

I looked at all three of these vile bastards; Sick Mick the psycho beast was looking up and smiling at me. I acknowledged his smile. He then put his blood-covered fist up to me and opened one finger. Very insulting... I slowly raised my gun and shot him right between the eyes!

I turned to the next one, the other lowlife scumbag Tomo. He had been lying there quietly and not saying a word, there was blood all around him. I nudged him with my foot, he didn't move... too bad.... he was already dead!

The last one was the Rat. I looked at him with hatred. He took it in turns to rape that young boy, and to me he is just as bad as the beast I've just got rid of.

He tried to bargain with me. 'Please, please don't kill me.' He pleaded. 'Let me go, let me go!'

I spoke to him coldly and slowly, 'You can't sell anything to me.' I raised my gun and my final words to him were, 'there's only one place you're going to.... Hell!'

I shot him in the forehead! It felt good and I thought to myself, *that's Justice*!

FINAL DECISION

I walked swiftly out of the room and up the stairs; I entered the front room, which had the lookout window. This time I put my head out and looked at the crowded street below me. It was packed tight. I saw ambulances on stand-by with police cars. I saw the TV satellite vans and the media also present. I looked again at the media presence and said to myself, it's funny; they will be the only ones who will gain anything from all this!

I put both of my hands out of the window; this was of course to let everybody see I was not armed. I knew they would have heard the three gunshots from inside of here. This then could have made some of the armed response team nervous and trigger-happy.

My next move was to start negotiations with the police voice but then thinking about it; there was nothing *to* negotiate, they had me bang to rights. Along the path I had taken during the past eighteen months; I was forever criticising the bizzies on how lackadaisical they were. I was the one who thought I knew it all, I even began to think I was infallible. Well I can hold my hands up now and say I underestimated them. I didn't know it at the time, but they had had me under their surveillance for weeks. I was now left with two choices; the first, I could give myself up and accept the life sentence that awaits me, if I did accept that fate I would never be set free and would die in prison. Alternatively I could end it all now... either by myself or a police bullet!

Then I remembered an old convict telling me years ago that *any* life is better than none.

I made my decision. I walked out and surrendered!

QUOTE FROM STEVE ON BEHALF OF THE VIGILANTES

I speak on behalf of myself and the rest of our circle:

John Christian to me was and still is a man of honour. He believed in old school values and was willing to help the underdog. Old ladies, men, women and kids when faced with today's lowlife scum in their communities sought John's help. After years of torment and abuse these clean decent people could finally sleep safely at night and begin to live their lives again. That is the man he is, a man who has principles to the core. Those who *did* break his code of honour... would live to regret it... others we now know, have died. In my opinion it was a justifiable act. Not only did those three evil scumbags, kidnap, torture and take it in turns to rape that young boy but it was a known fact that they carried out other sick acts on many more unfortunate people. To me, the way I see it and so do the majority of the public... those sick paedophiles got what was coming to them. Unfortunately due to this, a good and honourable man is to be incarcerated in prison for the rest of his life. At the present time myself and many other decent people have a petition in circulation, there are literally thousands of people who have signed it already, and that number is growing by the day, not just in Liverpool where it all began, but stretching over the whole country. I just hope to God those law officials whoever they are, make the right decision when they review and decide on this case, because I can sense anarchy and revolution in the air.

The public have been protesting for many years now concerning the leniency of the sentencing by judges of some of the vilest lowlife scum in this country. This is one of the main reasons decent people all over this country have now taken the law into their own hands and if those government officials don't take notice of this wakeup call and don't act immediately I am afraid there are going to be a lot more John Christian's dishing out justice.

QUOTE FROM A SENIOR POLICE OFFICER WHO INVESTIGATED THE CRIMES PAST AND PRESENT OF JOHN CHRISTIAN

I first heard the name John Christian many years ago. At that time as a police officer I was working in the serious crime squad. Merseyside over the years has produced a magnitude of violent and career criminals who were into heavy crime. During my time there we were dealing with what were known as target criminals. Names of these villains were often brought to our attention; one of the names mentioned was that of John Christian. His name was constantly coming up, every time an armed robbery or a violent crime was committed. He was known to be a careful planner and always seemed to provide a get out for himself. We had arrested him on several occasions but he always had an alibi, and every time he was charged he would always walk. Until, like every criminal who thinks crime pays, we finally got him convicted and he was sentenced to 10 years. On his release Christian then had a reputation for being a violent character. Intelligence was constantly being received of the most brutal violence perpetrated by this man; he had established himself by organising and controlling a gang of men who were known as vigilantes.

These so called vigilantes thought they had the God given right to take the law into their own hands and inflict the most dreadful of violent atrocities one could imagine on the young men they kidnapped. They then had the audacity to call it justice. At his trial he pleaded not guilty to three murders by self-defence but the evidence against him was overwhelming. He was the one who always criticised the judicial system and judges; believing the sentencing had become too lenient on, in his own words; lowlife scum and sexual abusers of women and children.

With the sentence he received this had backfired on him and was more than appropriate... Life.

Life, for one of the most dangerous men in Britain. Some of the public look up to this man for inspiration and others are calling him a *Hero*. How can this be? He shot dead three young men in cold blood. In my opinion he is just another ruthless criminal who has been taken off the streets. They named him a vigilante. This maybe so, but in the opinion of my colleagues and I, he was a cold blooded killer; a **Killer Vigilante!**

THE END

REVIEWS OF CHARLIE SEIGA'S OTHER BOOKS

'Streetwise'

After reading Charlie's first book Killer I couldn't wait to get my hands on this new title. I read it cover to cover without stopping for breath. The life story of Charlie's childhood years growing up in Liverpool and learning his criminal trade was both fascinating, funny and sad. This book left me crying and laughing at the true stories he tells page after page. I highly recommend this book as a must read!
Fred, Amazon Uk

A brilliant combination of narrative writing, memoir and biography.
Kevin Bryan, Publisher, Cumbria

Wow! What a read! After reading Charlie's first book Killer I couldn't wait to get my hands on this new title. I read it cover to cover without stopping for breath. The life story of Charlie's childhood years growing up in Liverpool and learning his criminal trade was both fascinating, funny and sad. This book left me crying and laughing at the true stories he tells page after page. I highly recommend this book as a must read!

'Fred20608'

Fabulously real narrative! A Kid's Review! Charlie's childhood could never be described as dull and ordinary. He and his family found themselves needing, and Charlie went out there and provide...any way he could! This book is a true gem. The descriptions of the environment in war torn Liverpool will ring bells for many others who suffered and lived through the hard times of yesteryear. And those who were lucky enough not to will get a unique insight into the true way it was! It is sensitive, moving, funny and truly entertaining. This wonderful book is a social history as well as an autobiography; real page turner and a story you can read again and again. It is not unlike a modern day Oliver Twist! Any money spent on buying this book will be money well spent. If only all autobiographies were this honest and raw straight from the horse's mouth. FABULOUS BOOK FABULOUS AUTHOR!!

A. Customer. Amazon

Fascinating! The early years autobiography of Charlie Seiga, one of Liverpool's most notorious criminals and author of 'Killers' and 'The Hyenas'. This fascinating book tells how his life of crime began and is in turn sensitive, moving, funny as

well as spelling out his villainous ways, always with a strict code of honour. A very scarce book.
Godley Books

The huckleberry fin of Liverpool! This book is such an unusual narrative for these days, as it is of a 'child' gangster for the want of a better word. Charlie Seiga was just 12 years old when he turned to crime to provide food and other basics for the large family he was from. He starts off just stealing food and sweets but then after meeting his mentor; a thirty odd year old woman who teaches him all she knows about blagging and thieving on a more lucrative level. Charlie Seiga writes about his younger years after writing his first book Killer and getting asked to write in more detail about his childhood. And so as requested here is A Liverpool Streetwise Kid...all the ups and downs, and sad and funny tails of the 'Huckleberry Fin' of Liverpool. Highly recommended. Buy it and read it, you won't be disappointed...5 Star!!!
A Customer

'The Hyenas'

I think you have a wonderful story to tell and that this autobiography will sell really strongly.......It's a great story, exciting and well written.
John Blake, *John Blake Publishing Limited.*

I think that this book is better than killer as it's much more relevant to today's society. It flows well and the characterization is really excellent. Hugely entertaining, but also quite shocking. Brutal but honest!....I am in Belmarsh Prison in May and I am using your book in the class, to give them an example of how to go about an autobiography.
Martina Cole, *author of multiple multinational crime fictions.*

A mesmerizing book that takes you beyond Killer. This final instalment brings you right up to the present day, with Charlie Siega's harrowing and brutal true tale. It truly is a 'can't put down' book.
A.Maxwell, writer and book critic.

This is the shocking story behind Charlie Siega's fate at the hands of the hyenas. The story takes you on an unmissable roller coaster of a ride from events which happened only a brief time ago. I couldn't put the book down and read from

start to finish nonstop, the chapters which describe the kidnapping and the following torture was like something out of a Hollywood movie, only this was for real! Having read **Charlie's last book** 'Killer', couldn't wait for this book to be released, but was well worth it. Would definitely recommend to buy this book, UNMISSABLE!
Neil Honey, St.Helens, Merseyside

Excellent! A must have! Couldn't put it down in any way it's truly inspiring and I would strongly advise it, can't wait for the next one.
P Hunt

<u>W</u>**ithout doubt is one of the most thrilling and well written crime books I have ever read**. Downloaded it at 11pm read it all and finished it at 4am the next morning. Impossible to put down. Once met him where we both live in West Derby, Liverpool with me a classic car enthusiast, asking him questions about his red Mercedes 107 SL sports car, which I think used to belong to Graham Souness the Liverpool FC footballer. He made it quite obvious he did not like me asking questions, so sensibly I made a quick exit. :-). I went to all the night clubs mentioned in the book and eventually I met my wife in the Victoriana when it was called the Downbeat in 1967. The book certainly made me reminisce and gave me a real feel of those amazing times of 60s

Merseybeat. Really looking forward to his next book. Keep up the good work Charlie and I promise I won't ask you questions about your cars :-).
Millie.

I could not put this book down. The books this author writes are well written easy to understand and hard to believe their not fiction stories. Your adventure begins once you pick any of his books up. This book is amazing what happens in Liverpool and the authors Gangster World. I would never agree to the extreme lengths of violence that gangsters of crime go too, and yet I seem to know where the author is coming from in his title Vigilantes book. I have also bought and absolutely enjoyed reading the authors other books, before you read this, buy Vigilantes, the author introduces you to his world, after reading this book you will find yourself understanding why the vicious beatings where necessary to prove a point. I could hear my heart racing whilst reading and getting involved in this book and felt myself turning a blind eye. I recommend this book as five stars.
Angie O

After reading Charlie's first book 'Killer' I was hooked and had to read the next one. Killer is a great, well-written autobiography about the life of crime resulting in the acquittal for murder and I couldn't see how the next book could improve. Well it did. And the story told is true.

In Killer Charlie tells us how he helped a fellow prisoner out while in prison while in The Hyenas this same prisoner was setting him up and on release kidnapped, tortured and was ready to kill him.

The Hyenas tells how Charlie was kidnapped and the viciousness of the torture that he received from the 'low life scum' that carried out this terrible crime. He was threatened with a knife and gun, bitten and beaten and boiling hot water thrown over him. This torture lasted 2 days before being released instead of murdered and he was only released because one of the kidnappers was seen taking Charlie away otherwise he would have been shot there and then. Followed by the trial where the 2 out of the 4 that were actually caught thought they would actually get away it and yet for all that excessive violence the maximum sentence handed down was 12 years!

A true story of a truly shocking, violent and senseless crime. No matter what you may think, heard or have read about Charlie Seiga this was totally undeserved and all for money. He was lucky to escape with his life.

Very well written and while telling this gruesome story Charlie shows the differences between the 'old time villains' who had respect, manners and honour (which Charlie still holds dear) to the vile low life of today who would rob a pensioner using extreme violence for their last £1.

Along with the crimes he has committed, it also shows his good side in helping old neighbours who were terrified of being robbed by giving them his phone number in case they were frightened and fitting locks to their doors.

Overall, another very powerful book by Charlie Seiga. A gripping read from start to finish. Yes, he has admitted to crimes and whatever you may think about the moral issues of villains and gangsters profiting from their crimes by writing books this one is worth every penny, very well written and is a true account of his life and the vile things done to him because of crime.

If you want a proper true crime book then I recommend reading Charlie's books, they are extremely well written, absorbing and entertaining. If you only buy one book this year make it one by Charlie Seiga, you will not disappointed. I could not put it down.
D J Savage 'whatsgoodtodo.com'

'Killer'

This is an excellent piece of original writing. Charlie has natural story-telling style, and the reader's interest is maintained throughout. The story is structured well, with a detailed introduction, creating plenty of period atmosphere. It is developed into an exciting narrative. Writing as he thinks and speaks makes the story more authentic and realistic. Keep on writing!

Alan, Manchester

After reading your brilliant book Killer, I am convinced that your story would make a compelling film. Charlie is a man who has done a lot of things in his life, always for good reason; in his eyes. The way I see it; he is no angel..... then again; he is no devil either..... we'll leave it at that! One thing for sure is that he is a gentleman. Recently, I had to go to Liverpool, and Charlie and his friends met me. There was a limo waiting at the station, and I have to say that I was treated like a princess. Maybe it's called Liverpool hospitality; I'm not sure. Devil? Killer? But gentleman?...Definitely!

Kate Kray, crime writer and wife of the notorious late Ronnie Kray

A wonderful and moving account of the trials and struggles of one good man, in a world full of unsavoury characters. This is arguably the finest 'peace, justice and the American way' genre book ever written. It moved me to tears. The best criminals are the ones who write books about crime and stuff in my honest opinion. The author was no angel. His struggle forced him into crime. He attempted to bring down the system from within and very nearly brought it off. A great book. Buy it and read.
W Findlay (USA), Rated five stars on Amazon

I believe 'Killer' will be a major television six part drama. It is a very powerful story and I wouldn't rule out a major film theatrical production.
Colin McKeown, Liverpool producer
(whose works include Nice Guy Eddie and Liverpool one).

This book brought back memories of growing up in a hard environment; one could turn to crime or make good at school. One had to fight or be walked over. Charlie tells it as it was with no holds barred. He took to crime to fulfil his dreams. I worked in the local factory as a slave to industry. Many people will relate to this book; as it describes the pressures put on people trying to make a living, honestly or dishonestly. Charlie believed in certain 'old fashioned values' and was willing to help the underdog. Old ladies did not go in fear of Charlie, in fact they sought his help when faced with today's drug inspired yobs. This book will be read by many all over the world who will recognise similar people in their own back yard.

BF, Liverpool, Five star rating

This true tale has shed a different light on the old school gangsters. Life in Liverpool through the heart of a gentleman that decided the life of crime might be for him; living by a code of honour that has disappeared in the villains of today. Confronted by bullies of the weak, Charlie took it upon himself to stand up and help; unlike society today. This book was written whilst Charlie awaits trial for the murder of a local career criminal (taxer of weaker criminals). From the first temptation through the roller-coaster of emotions, that has that can't put it down feeling. This taught my three teenage sons (who all read this within 24 hrs, first time) that the true to life is different from the Hollywood videos and is off putting to leading a life of crime. Words struggle to describe how gripping the book is. A real eye-opener to the underworld that has hilarious scams and illegal jobs that go right and wrong. All to earn a buck! This autobiography out rates the various fact & fiction 'best-sellers' I have ever read in my life. If all 5 star reading was this good I better get a bigger book case! As if!

James Bett, Scotland

My parents are in their sixties and enjoyed this book as much as I did; me being in my early twenties. The book itself would be a delight to read even without the dramatic impact of the violence; as it covers the great generations of the last century. In my opinion this book stands out from the categories it is placed in, and it deserves a better title than 'Killer' as this limits the book far too much. Read it and you will agree.

S Smart, Liverpool John Moores University

I had the honour of meeting Charlie Seiga and subsequently read his book. Let me clarify that; this was one book that I just couldn't put down. The insight into life in Liverpool, and the life of a latter day Robin Hood, made this one of the best books I have ever read. Charlie told me he is writing another one. Hurry up and do so Charlie, this is one book waiting for a place on my shelf. Charlie is one of the most charismatic, talented and amusing men I have ever had the honour to meet.

A Customer, Amazon, Uk

Master Criminal, scouser; Charlie Seiga leads us on a rollicking rumbustuous ride
through his life of crime and his dealings with blaggers, ponses, narks and the like.
Throughout his career as a villain, Charlie is seen to retain the values of integrity,
candour and humour, whichever difficult situation he finds himself in. His dry wit and straight talking style transfers itself beautifully to the page, making a common-or-garden novel about thieving and murder, rise above anything else currently on the shelves. A unique insight into a life lived on the 'other side of the tracks'. Stop whatever you are doing. Go out. Buy it.

Trinnie Murgatroyd, Barrow-In-Furness

Different! A good crime read, which will be of particular interest to those in and around Liverpool. There are perhaps better books around but this is worth a look if you are bored with the usual 'celebrity villains'.

Mr.M.Knight.(Lancashire)

Hurry up and write the next one! I had the honour of meeting Charlie Seiga and subsequently read his book. Let me clarify that - this was one book that I just couldn't put down. The insight into life in Liverpool and the life of a latter day Robin Hood made this one of the best books I have ever read. Charlie told me he is writing another one. Hurry up and do so Charlie, this is one book waiting for a place on my shelf. Charlie is one of the most charismatic, talented and amusing men I have ever had the honour to meet.

A Customer, AmazonUK

Best author of the true crime genre! This is another sublime narrative from Charlie Seiga. I have read all his books now and am waiting with much anticipation for another. He manages to grab the reader from the first page, then you cannot stop, a real page turner. He doesn't glam up the violence written about, he shows the soft and gentle side of his nature too. He just doesn't suffer fools and hates men who treat women and children with little or no respect...rapist and child abusers and the like. I would recommend this book to anyone, not just those who like to read this genre of book but anyone who is in the market for a good, honest entertaining read. He comes across as an intelligent gentleman with verve and energy and empathy but also

humorous, clever and witty...though obviously if you are a child molester or woman beater, he is a very dangerous unforgiving man!
A Customer, AmazonUK

Great read! A great read there are a couple more in the collection which I now have completed reading you will not want to put it down (wouldn't argue with this guy)
Derek, Reader

I read Killer the other week, enjoyed it, once I picked it up I didn't put it down; which is always a sign of a good read!
P Hunt, Worcester

'The Jelly Gang'
Excellent new book from one of my favourite writers. Charlie Seiga's new book about his early days as part of a robbery crew. This is a great addition to Charlie's other books about the start of his life in crime. It tells how due to an idea of Charlie's the gang became quite innovative in safe blowing. A must for any Charlie Seiga fan and a great addition to any true crime library.
The Mechanic

Five Stars. Absolutely fantastic!!
Barry. Amazon customer

I didn't even know what a Jelly Gangs was until I read this new Charlie Seiga book. I do now; it's a safe blower!! He was only 17 when he came up with the idea of using gelignite to blow safes open and told his brother and the gang that it was the way forward! I couldn't put this book down as I wanted to find out what happened to him and his gang. The story of each character makes you care about them. Great story and I bet there's no one else that could write a story like this one. Great!
J Somerville Doncaster

Wow what a read the jelly gang as they were known I couldn't put this book down from start to finish Liverpool safe crackers in the early years of the 1950s so exciting and fascinating I am only in by early twenties and the life and times then must have been. It's not just about criminals safe blowing it's about how they lived and what the fashions were and the music in the charts at the time.... I wish I had lived then!!!
Diane. Manchester

A Brief Synopsis of Charlie Seiga's other books

A STREETWISE KID

By Charlie Seiga

Times were hard in the 1940's and early 1950's. Kids went hungry and food was rationed. Some families had to beg, steal or borrow to survive. There seemed no way out for some kids, but Charlie found his own way out. On a routine basis he and his child gang plundered every shop they came across, robbing them of their food to put on the family table and their goods to sell on. At the age of thirteen and always bunking off school, he went on to make further progress in his way of life. With his baby face and dressed as an office boy in blazer, shirt and tie, he was darting in and out of the office buildings in the city centre of Liverpool, raiding their cash draws and safes.

Quote from Charlie: 'We had one of the best little firms in Huyton, we got up to all kinds of things; fighting, robbery, you name it. Nobody could stop us or so I thought. I was scared of nothing and of nobody; especially the bizzies (police). In 1954 and at the tender age of fourteen I was earning more money than a professional adult. I was the richest, poor teenager in Liverpool.'

A Streetwise Kid is a brilliant combination of narrative writing, memoir and biography. A true story of a childhood villain and his young gang growing up in war torn Liverpool.

KILLER

By Charlie Seiga

Charlie Seiga was one of the most dangerous faces of the criminal underworld. There were many unsolved killings which were swift brutal and brilliantly organised. The victims - liberty takers and sadists – were all hard bastards who dealt in the most vicious kind of violence. Many times the police marked him out as the vicious contract killer.

He was also one of the most successful villains of his time. Police believed that he was the brains behind major firms involved in robberies on banks, security vans, lorry hijacking, safe breaking and many other serious crimes. He lost track of the times he was arrested and questioned about various jobs, but he always had an alibi – a witness to say he wasn't guilty of the crime. He was the Houdini of the criminal underworld.

His story is a shocking tale of violence and crime; but it is also a story about one man's fight against the scum who break his deadly code of honour. He hates women beaters and child molesters. His presence was a constant challenge to the low life that preyed on those who could not defend themselves.

It is an incredible autobiography of one of the most notorious figures in the history of British crime.

'...LIKE WALKING INTO A SCENE FROM THE GOODFELLAS'
LOADED

'CHILLING AND COMPLETELY ABSORBING'
SUNDAY PEOPLE

THE HYENAS

By Charlie Seiga

'I was in constant pain. My back had been bitten and torn by one of those crazy animals. Boiling water had been slowly poured over parts of my body and the skin was blistering and peeling off. I was screaming in agony and cursing them at the same time. I thought they had finished torturing me... then they strapped me tightly to a chair. The blood was running down my face from the knife wound which was done as they had threatened to follow by cutting my eyes out. Nearly two days had passed since that perverted, sick bastard, Lea, had mutilated my body.

'Charlie, we respect you as a man.' said one of them ominously. 'but you know who we are.' I immediately knew this was the end, they were ready to kill me...'

The stories I had heard about these people were sickening. I thought I had seen them at their worst, but this just made me more and more determined to get my revenge on these dogs, I don't care what I have to do or how long it takes.

THE JELLY GANG

By Charlie Seiga

Charlie Seiga was young, fearless and ambitious; he craved the good things life had to offer. At the age of just seventeen he led a gang of older men into doing daring safe blowing robberies up and down the country using high explosives (gelignite). This story tells, in intricate detail, all about the methods used in safe blowing and how professional these men were at the business they chose to be involved in. They became known as 'The Jelly Gang.'

At that time; back in the 1950s, safe blowing was regarded as the pinnacle of excellence amongst the gangsters of that era. It demanded a superior knowledge and technique and required meticulous planning of the highest degree. Expertise in the way explosives worked was paramount. Although on some occasions it was a very dangerous game to be in and there was near death, disaster and injuries in some of the moves the Jelly Gang pulled off.

They knew how to make plenty of money and in doing so they led a fast and privileged lifestyle sampling the best money could buy.

Whilst they carried out these audacious and daring raids they managed to evade capture by always being one step ahead of the police. Police forces throughout the country were well aware of the Jelly Gang and each police force wanted to be the one that would successfully bring them down.

However, it was inevitable that their luck would only last for so long.

In 1958 the youth was standing in the dock of the Crown Court flanked on both sides by the older members of his gang. The judge, directing his words towards the youth was quoted as saying; 'He is like a young lion who had tasted his first blood.' He made legal history by becoming the youngest and first safe blower in England.

This is also the true personal story of the characters involved; how they became what they were and how they lived, some retiring and living a comfortable life and others sadly not so lucky.

The Jelly Gang is a brilliant combination of narrative writing, memoir and biography.